Enterprise Architecture for Developers, IT/Dev Ops, Architects, Designers, Business analysts, Managers & Executives

Author information

For any help please contact :
Amazon Author Page :
amazon.com/author/ajaykumar
Email : ajaycucek@gmail.com ,
Linkedin :
https://www.linkedin.com/in/ajaycucek
Facebook :
https://www.facebook.com/ajaycucek
Youtube :
 https://www.youtube.com/channel/UC1uXE
ebtqCLYxVdzirKZGIA
Twitter : https://twitter.com/ajaycucek
Instagram :
https://www.instagram.com/ajaycucek/

Table of contents

Module:1 Introducing Enterprise Architecture

Introduction

In this book we will explore the contours of enterprise architecture.
Book Caters to a Wide Spectrum of Audience

- Developers
- IT/ Dev Ops Professionals
- Architects and Designers
- Business Analysts
- Project/ Program Managers
- Enterprise Architects
- Senior Managers and Executives

The book caters to a wide spectrum of audience. These include developers, IT and DevOps professionals, architects and designers, business analysts, project and program managers, enterprise architects, senior managers and executives, typically within medium to large enterprises. So let's jump straight into the subject and get some of the basics out of the way by answering some initial questions that comes up in our mind.

- What is an Enterprise?
- What is Architecture?
- Why Enterprise Architecture?
- Why Should You Care?

What exactly do we mean by an enterprise? What do we mean by architecture? And why does an enterprise require architecture? And finally, why should you care, and what can you hope to gain from this book?

What Is an Enterprise?

- A single organization
- Parts of a large organization (such as a business unit)
- A collection of organizations collaborating in a value stream
- The word "Enterprise" covers a broad spectrum of organizational entities

Well, an enterprise can be a single organization, a part of a large organization such as the business unit that is accountable for say a function like HR, sales, customer service, etc, or it could be a collection of a number of organizations that work together and contribute towards producing something of value and making it accessible for people who consume it. This definition covers a broad spectrum of organizational entities of all sizes and shapes including private corporations, government agencies, armed forces, profit and non-profit organizations, and so forth. Now that we have quickly glanced over what an enterprise means, now let's look at architecture.

Etymological Analysis of Architecture

- ARCHITECT --> ArchitectÉ -->> ARKHITECTON --> Arkhi = Chief Tecton = Builder -->>
- Master Builder
- Architecture is the craft of the master builders
- Enterprise Architecture can be interpreted as the craft of creating a blueprint of execution for the enterprise

What does architecture mean? Well, etymologically, the root word architect can be traced back to the word architecte in Middle French, which eventually can be traced back to the Greek word of antifirst is arkhi meaning chief in a sense of how we use it in English in words such as matriarch, patriarch, et cetera. And the word tecton means builder. So if you put them together as in arkhitecton, it seems to take the meaning of chief builder or, in other words, master builder, and hence in the context of the Greek civilization at least, architecture is the craft of the master builders. Purely from an etymological perspective, enterprise architecture can therefore be interpreted as the craft of creating a master plan or a blueprint of an enterprise. Well, that would be really an oversimplification if we leavquity, arkhitecton. It turns out that this Greek word, arkhitecton, is composed of two words. The e it at that.

- Enterprises Are Complex Adaptive Systems
- Architects are engaged usually when the enterprise is already functional
- In other words, enterprise architects deal with systems that are constantly acting, reacting and evolving in reaction to its environment

An enterprise is often referred to as a complex adaptive system. That is, by the time architects are usually engaged to architect an enterprise, the enterprises that they are architecting are already functional and are constantly acting on and changing in reaction to its environment. Hence, unlike in the case of building or a physical structure, the blueprints of an enterprise should embrace constant change and dynamism while at the same time guiding and enabling the enterprise to meet its vision and strategic objectives.

Why Do We Need Enterprise Architecture?

- Historically, it emerged as a mechanism to handle the complexity of IT systems implementation
- Along the way the role of EA transformed to address the architecture of the whole of the enterprise rather than just the IT components

But why do enterprises need architecture? Well, historically, it emerged from the need to gain a handle on the complexity of their current IT systems implementations and to clear the road map to declutter IT systems. Somewhere along the way though, the role of enterprise architecture transformed to address the whole of the enterprise rather than just the IT components of the enterprise. Later, in a subsequent section of this module, we will be going through the enterprise architecture's evolution timeline and the definition of what an EA is. We shall talk about this transition in more details.

Why Should You Care?

It Depends …

- Developer, System Admin, System/ Business Analyst
- Project/ Program Managers
- Technical/ Solutions Architect
- Enterprise Architect
- Senior Executives & Managers

Lastly, why should you care and what is in this book for you? The answer is it depends really on your interests and perhaps the current role you're playing in your organization and perhaps the career paths you're choosing to explore. If you are a developer, systems administrator, systems or business analyst, enterprise architecture could be an interesting career direction that you can work towards if you are interested in moving into more strategic roles that works with the big picture and enables large-scale transformation initiatives within your organization. If you are a project or program manager or anyone working within a team and interacting with an architect, a good understanding of enterprise architecture will help you better understand architectural perspectives and help you to have deeper and meaningful conversations with an architect. If you are already a technical architect focused on implementations or a solutions architect creating solutions that span across multiple systems and business units, you are most likely to be already familiar with the

aspects of enterprise architecture; however, this book could provide you with good grounding that consolidates your understanding and completes the picture for you. If you are already an enterprise architect, use this book as a refresher on the concepts and to keep updated on the current thinking and views on this subject area. If you are a senior manager or a senior executive within an organization, this book provides you an understanding of what enterprise architecture has to offer and how you can use it as a strategic tool.

Objectives of This Module :

- A working definition of enterprise architecture
- Overview of the modules of the book

This first module has two very simple objectives. First, to provide a working definition of the enterprise architecture that serves as a reference and provides a contextual framework that we refer back to as we go through the rest of the modules in this book. The other objective is to provide a quick walkthrough of the modules of this book so that you can design your own journey through the

book as guided by your interest in specific topics. Although the book by itself is laid out in a logical sequence that probably suits most of the target
audience, I encourage you to customize and make this journey your own. With that said, we're just about to jump into the details and the nitty-gritties of enterprise architecture.

EA - Historical Perspective

Enterprise Architecture Has Many Facets
- EA limited to enterprise IT architecture
- EA is enterprise-wide solutions architecture
- EA as a tool for business – IT alignment EA as a discipline for architecting business capabilities and functions

There are many different facets of enterprise architecture that you can come across in the marketplace. The perspectives on enterprise architecture of each individual organization may vary slightly or even vastly, and it may vary even within an organization depending on who you talk to. In this section, we will explore some of the reasons why this happens. Some of the views I have encountered in my consulting gigs include enterprise architecture as enterprise IT architecture. That is, according to this viewpoint, enterprise architecture is entirely about architecting IT infrastructure and IT systems. Another common perspective is enterprise architecture refers to enterprise-wide solutions architecture. This is a view held by some organization which views enterprise architecture as a discipline for effectively architecting enterprise solutions. Some others view enterprise architecture as a tool for aligning business strategies and IT initiatives. And another common perspective is to view enterprise architecture as a tool for architecting business capabilities and functions of the enterprise. Such a variety of viewpoints makes defining enterprise architecture quite a daunting task in the first glance. It might be worth taking a quick peek at the origin and the brief history of enterprise architecture to understand the plurality of perspectives in the marketplace.

Historical View

- IT initiatives and spending have been historically tactical and operational, directed at solving an immediate problem
- This attitude to IT systems resulted in a clutter of technology implementations
  - Spaghetti relationships
  - High level of redundancies
  - Systems cross-purpose with each other

Historically, the role of IT began as a back office function enabling businesses to efficiently process computation- intensive tasks primarily around finance and accounting functions in most cases. Although strategy in general as a business concept took root in the industry in the 70s and 80s, historically IT initiatives and spend have traditionally been tactical and operational and directed at solving an immediate problem at hand. This attitude to IT systems resulted in a clutter of technology implementations with high levels of redundancies and even systems that have cross-purpose with each other essentially contributing to what is referred to in some quarters as the Hairball Architecture. This problem got further aggravated as IT systems took center stage and represented the key capabilities and platforms for the enterprise to build competitive differentiation.

EA - Making Sense of Plurality of Perspectives

One thing that is obvious from this timeline overview of enterprise architecture is that the reality that the businesses are facing today is significantly different from what the businesses faced in the 1960s and 70s. This is simply because of the nature of the problems and the opportunities that they are dealing with and the overall environment in which they operate. The business models, the markets, the supply and distribution chains, the customer expectations, the behaviors and how they access product and services, the technology that is accessible and available to the enterprise, as well as the globalized competitive business landscape of today's knowledge economy are significantly different from that of the business reality of the Industrial Age of 70s and 80s and the Information Age that took off in the 90s. In fact, many analysts believe that post global financial crisis of 2007, 2008, businesses have grown increasingly dynamic and complex reflecting the increasing dynamism in the business environment. The role of information systems and information technology as a whole took many unexpected turns along the way going from being primarily a back office computational and number crunching function to becoming a foundational and core competency which shapes, drives, and evolves

the business forward in many of the industries.
The pace of such changes are only accelerating
and spreading wider. Enterprise architecture at
different eras attempted to solve different
challenges faced by the enterprise in that era.
And although it began primarily as an IT
architecture discipline, along the way it evolved
into something that enabled bridging strategic
business objectives and IT initiatives,
and further along into a discipline that can be
used to architect the whole of the enterprise.

- Enterprises are like cities; they evolve
  and modernize balancing the old and the
  new
- EA practice is evolving keeping pace
  with the needs of an evolving enterprise

Enterprise architecture metaphorically is often
compared to the master plan of a city and like
how cities of antiquity adopting modern design
facilities, capabilities, and infrastructure are
having to continuously reinvent themselves and
merge and balance the old with the new.
Similarly, most enterprises are having to do the
same driven by either forward-thinking vision
or out of necessity and compulsion. To enable a
fast-evolving enterprise, the enterprise
architecture practice itself is constantly
evolving to tackle newer problems, as well as
take advantage of new opportunities.

Evolution Continuum

- A given enterprise's EA practice
  occupies a certain range in the EA
  evolution continuum
- This depends on many factors such as:
  - The enterprise's history of
    adopting EA practice
  - Individuals leading the practice

- The kinds of problems and opportunities the enterprise is tackling
- The leadership's view on how it can leverage EA

Given that old view of the history of enterprise architecture, a given enterprise's EA practice typically occupies a certain range in the overall continuum of the EA evolution. This depends on the factors such as the organization's history of adopting EA, the individuals manning and leading the enterprise architecture capability within the organization, and the kinds of problems their enterprise is attempting to tackle using enterprise architecture. This view is also informed by the leadership's perspective on what EA is and their understanding of how they can leverage enterprise architecture for executing strategies.

Defining Enterprise Architecture

- Enterprise Architecture Enterprise
- Architecture is a discipline which enables designing the enterprise consciously and deliberately, rather than letting it happen randomly.
- The design is informed by business vision, strategic intent and insights on the functioning of the enterprise.

Now we are at the stage in the module where we can actually go ahead and define enterprise architecture. So let's look at a practical definition. Enterprise architecture is a discipline which enables designing the enterprise consciously and deliberately, rather than letting it happen randomly. This design is informed by business vision, strategic intent, and insights on the functioning of the enterprise.

- The purpose of EA is to enable consciously designing your enterprise
- When we say Design, it implies knowledge of a certain intended outcome or desired state

So as per this definition, the purpose of enterprise architecture is very clear. It is to be able to consciously design your enterprise rather than allowing it to happen randomly and unconsciously. It is worth noting that when we say design, it implies knowledge of a certain intended outcome or desired state in mind. This is usually referred to as the target state.

Target State

- Target state is defined by attainment of capabilities and fulfillment of milestones
- Target state is informed by business vision, strategic intent and insights
- Vision and strategic intent conveys the top-down holistic view of the enterprise direction
- Vision and mission are relatively static
- Strategy evolves continuously in response to stimulus from business environments
- Insights represent the knowledge of the functioning of the enterprise

The target state is defined in terms of the attainment of certain capabilities and fulfillment of certain milestones. The other aspect of this definition is about what informs our concept of a desired target state, which the definition clarifies to be a business vision, strategic intent, and insights. Vision and strategic intent implies a top-down holistic view of the enterprise and a good understanding of the direction that the enterprise wants to move in. It is important to note that while the vision and mission of an enterprise are usually static, this strategy and strategic objectives continually evolve in response to the emerging business scenarios. The insights part of the definition represent the knowledge and understanding of the details of the working of the enterprise and how various capabilities, resources, and

components that the enterprise relies on comes together to deliver business value.

- EA provides frameworks, tools, viewpoints and perspectives to comprehend, the current state, articulate the target state and enables road-mapping the journey from current to target state

Enterprise architecture provides various frameworks, tools, viewpoints, and perspectives to first comprehend the enterprise in its current state and also to consciously design and articulate target state enterprise that best meets its vision, mission, and strategic objectives. It also involves road-mapping the journey to the target state.

- The outcome of EA is not merely a repository of artefacts
- The results are in the real change within the enterprise
- KPI of EA is the positive and beneficial impacts of these changes
- EA therefore implies not just creating documents and blueprints, but active collaboration to bring changes to life

That stated, it is important to note that the outcome of the result of enterprise architecture is not merely a repository of artifacts, but the introduction of real change within the enterprise which is in alignment with its strategic objectives and tactical priorities. The KPI of enterprise architecture is therefore the positive impacts resulting out of these changes and the achievement of strategic objectives. While enterprise architecture involves creating many artifacts in the book of the architecture work, the purpose of architecture will not be met unless these artifacts influence and guide how the enterprise evolves and changes. To this end, enterprise architecture work involves not only documentation, but also active involvement and collaboration across the enterprise capabilities and stakeholders.

- Enterprises Are Complex Adaptive Systems
- Complex Adaptive Systems (CAS) are systems characterized by complex behaviors that result from non-linear interactions among large number of components in time and space at various levels of organization

Also, it is worth keeping in mind that enterprises are complex adaptive systems where a complex adaptive system is defined as systems that are characterized by complex behaviors that emerge as a result of non-linear interactionsin space and time among a large number of component systems at different levels of organization. Other often cited examples of complex adaptive systems include the brain, immune system, societies, and ecosystems. By definition, complex adaptive systems are not a sum of its parts and hence an atomistic view of an enterprise. That is a view of the enterprise arrived at by breaking it down into smaller units of organization may be useful in comprehending each individual part and how they fit into the larger whole, but it will not lead to a holistic understanding of the enterprise itself. To use an analogy, for example, if you get two cars, one from UK and the one from US, and break it apart and understand it in terms of their components, that analysis might answer some questions about the functioning of these cars, but that analysis alone will not tell you why one has the steering wheel on the left side and the other has it on the right side. An automobile is not just a sum of its parts. If it was so, hypothetically you can replace each individual component of an automobile with the best components in the world, and you could end up with the best engineered automobile in the world. But we all know that if we do that, we probably will end up with a lot of junk on our hands.

- Understanding the component parts does not lead to the full understanding of the whole Inter-connectivity, interactions and inter-relationships give rise to complexity

The complexity of a complex adaptive system emerges from the inter-connectivity, interactions, and inter-relationships among the components, which is very true in the case of an enterprise.

Enterprise Architecture Embraces Both Atomistic & Holistic Views

- Atomistic View <<------------------------ >>Holistic View

Hence, the enterprise architecture discipline incorporates both atomistic and holistic view of the enterprise.

Overview of Modules

Enterprise Architecture Domains

- Business Architecture
- Information Systems Architecture
  - Applications Architecture
  - Information Architecture
- Technology (Infrastructure) Architecture

In general, enterprise architecture views are classified into the following domains: business architecture, information systems architecture, which comprises both applications architecture and information architecture, technology architecture, and the contours of the present book are roughly based on this categorization. Following is a quick view of what the book has to offer.

Module Overview

- Module 1 – Introduction to EA/ Course Overview
- Module 2 – EA Frameworks
- Module 3 - Business Architecture
- Module 4 – Applications Architecture
- Module 5 – Information Architecture
- Module 6 – Infrastructure Architecture
- Module 7 – Other Architecture Disciplines
- Module 8 – Enterprise Architecture Roles
- Module 9 – Agile & Enterprise Architecture

Module one is current module, which introduced the basic concepts of enterprise architecture and offered a working definition of EA and this overview of the book itself. The next module, which is the second module, provides an overview of enterprise architecture frameworks. It covers some of the popular frameworks in the market that are related to enterprise architecture. The module then offers guidance on their use in various scenarios.

Subsequently, module three introduces business architecture, the business case for it, that is the problems it addresses and opportunities and value it presents to the business, a working definition of it, and some of the methods and conceptual tools that are used to capture and represent business architecture. In module four, we introduce applications architecture and elaborate on the significance of having a deliberate applications portfolio strategy for the enterprise. It also looks at the current and future trends in this
space to get an understanding of the forces that are driving and shaping the evolution of applications architecture. Module five introduces the principle of using information as an enterprise asset and signifies the opportunity presented through strategic deployment of this principle across the enterprise through information architecture. Module six explores the technology or the infrastructure component of the enterprise architecture, and it offers a quick roundup of the key building blocks of the infrastructure component and also explores the future trends and directions in this space. Having covered the key domains of enterprise architecture between modules three to six, module seven covers some of the other specialized architecture practice areas emerging within the enterprise such as cloud, big data, and social enterprise, et cetera. Module eight offers guidance on architecture roles within the enterprise from the perspective of their scope of responsibilities, what outcomes and supporting artifacts they work with, who they particularly interact with, and what value do each of the roles have to offer. Module nine explores the role of enterprise architecture practice in the emerging turbulent business environments and

how the practice contributes towards enterprise agility while at the same time how it itself is evolving from the traditional ivory tower practice to being a collaborative hands-on and agile practice that supports enterprise-wide innovation.

Module:2
Enterprise Architecture Frameworks

Introduction to EA Frameworks

In this module, we will cover enterprise architecture frameworks. So, what are frameworks? For the purpose of illustration, consider the periodic table of elements, a simple one-pager that represents all known elements to mankind. The table uses simple principles such as the atomic number, electron configurations, and recurring chemical properties to organize them. This organizing framework makes it easy for someone who is looking up the elements in the table to infer a great deal about it just by looking at its position within the periodic table. It is not too farfetched to say that studying the elements without the organizing principles, such as the ones used in periodic table, can become too onerous very quickly.

- Frameworks are tools that help us organize concepts, knowledge, thinking and codify collective experience

- They enable quicker and easier comprehension domains as well as consistent communication
- EA can be quite daunting to practice in the absence of the organizing frameworks
- EA frameworks help by organizing concepts, principles, artefacts, processes, templates, reference models etc.
- EA frameworks enable effective collaboration with a wide spectrum of stakeholders

In generic terms, frameworks can be thought of as tools to help us organize concepts, knowledge, and thinking, and codify our collective experience of working in a domain into a condensed form that helps the practitioners to comprehend the domain quickly and communicate and collaborate effectively and consistently. Enterprise architecture can be quite daunting to practice in the absence of standardized frameworks that can be used for creating and communicating architectural models. An enterprise architecture framework helps by enabling the enterprise architecture practitioners to organize their concepts, principles, artifacts, processes, templates, reference models, et cetera as they work to collaborate with various teams and stakeholders to fulfill the enterprise architecture objectives and responsibilities. EA frameworks enables classification and organization of different models facilitating better access to different viewpoints and perspectives at levels of details appropriate for a wide spectrum of enterprise stakeholders. Some frameworks even provide more elaborate constructs to facilitate architecture development within the enterprise.

- Frameworks tend to have a lot of influence on how EA is practiced in the industry today
- This module will provide a quick overview of two of the popular EA frameworks
- The objective here is to provide overview of key concepts

Frameworks tend to have a lot of influence on how enterprise architecture is practiced in the industry today; hence, this module will attempt to provide a quick overview of two of the popular enterprise architecture frameworks. It is, however, important to note that the objective here is not to provide an exhaustive coverage of each framework, but rather to provide an overview of key concepts and characteristics in order to provide a high-level understanding of what they offer.

Focus of This Module

- Zachman Framework
- TOGAF (The Open Group Architecture Framework)

Specifically, we will be looking at the following enterprise frameworks. Zachman Framework, which is one of the popular and among the first enterprise architecture frameworks created. TOGAF, which stands for The Open Group Architecture Framework, and it is a very elaborate enterprise architecture framework and one which is gaining wide adoption in the industry.

Zachman Framework

Let's look at Zachman Framework first, which is referred to as the enterprise architecture ontology where an ontology is an mechanism which allows practitioners to manage complexity through compartmentalization and categorization and ordering. This is comparable to how elements are ordered within sections of periodic tables based on some principles and the properties they exhibit.

- Zachman framework is a metamodel, it provides a model of a model
- It essentially enables compartmentalizing the concepts, information, processes, viewpoints and perspectives required to articulate and model an enterprise's architecture

Zachman Framework is a metamodel. That is, it provides a model of a model. It essentially enables compartmentalizing the concepts, information, processes, viewpoints, and perspectives required to articulate and model an enterprise's architecture.

	Why (Motivation)	How (Process Flows)	What (Inventory Sets)	Who (Responsibility Assignments)	Where (Distribution Networks)	When (Timing Cycles)
Executive Perspective						
Business Mgmt. Perspective						
Architect Perspective						
Engineer Perspective						
Technician Perspective						
Enterprise Perspective						

It does so by using a two- dimensional matrix where the rows represent what is referred to as the reification transformations, which offers perspectives that are delivered for certain category of stakeholders where reification is the concept of transforming an idea into real instantiations using whatever is necessary, such as people, process, hardware, software, networks, and so forth. The columns of the matrix represent the architectural aspects of the system that essentially answers the five W's and the H questions, that is the why, what, who, where, when, and how, which are fundamental to understanding any system. The framework natively incorporates six rows representing different perspectives. Put together, these columns and rows covers 36 cells, each representing the intersection between an interrogative and a perspective which collectively define the architecture of the enterprise.

It might be worth noting that there are no implicit ordering for the columns as they represent different architectural aspects which are required for completing the architectural representation for each category of stakeholders. However, the framework does imply a top-down ordering of rows where the top row of layer represent the very high-level context of the enterprise, which gets progressively detailed and elaborated as you traverse down the rows. Which is not to say that one level is more important than the others, but essentially it provides the levels of abstraction suitable for different categories of stakeholders.

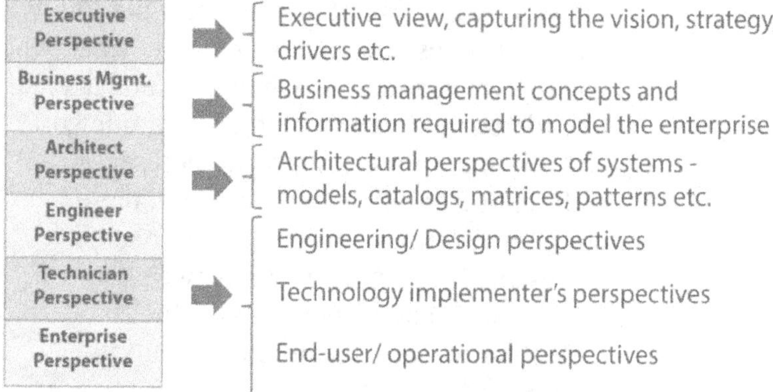

Taking a closer look at the application of Zachman Framework for enterprise architecture, we can see the top row caters essentially to executive perspectives and ensures that the architecture model of the enterprise captures the vision, strategy, strategic objectives, the drivers, the timeline, and all of the broad parameters to set the direction for the architecture planning. The row below that captures the business management concepts, and beneath that is the conceptual or the architectural perspectives followed by three detailed perspectives catering to the engineering or the designer's perspectives, technician or the implementer's perspectives, and finally the end user and operational perspectives.

	Why (Motivation)	How (Process Flows)	What (Inventory Sets)	Who (Responsibility Assignments)	Where (Distribution Networks)	When (Timing Cycles)
Executive Perspective	Motivation Identification	Process Identification	Inventory Identification	Responsibility Identification	Distribution Identification	Timing Identification
Business Mgmt. Perspective	Motivation Definition	Process Definition	Inventory Definition	Responsibility Definition	Distribution Definition	Timing Definition
Architect Perspective	Motivation Representation	Process Representation	Inventory Representation	Responsibility Representation	Distribution Representation	Timing Representation
Engineer Perspective	Motivation Specification	Process Specification	Inventory Specification	Responsibility Specification	Distribution Specification	Timing Specification
Technician Perspective	Motivation Configuration	Process Configuration	Inventory Configuration	Responsibility Configuration	Distribution Configuration	Timing Configuration
Enterprise Perspective	Motivation Instantiations	Process Instantiations	Inventory Instantiations	Responsibility Instantiations	Distribution Instantiations	Timing Instantiations

Hence, based on Zachman Framework, an enterprise architect capturing the architecture of say a retail organization and wanting to capture the physical outlets of the organization might capture it in an artifact which would then be locatable within the architecture repository under the section corresponding to the business management perspective and the where interrogative. Similarly, you can expect to find artifacts capturing the key architectural drivers of the enterprise architecture at the intersection of architecture perspective and the why interrogative.

Introducing TOGAF Framework

Zachman Framework, which we just covered, is both an ontology and a metamodel, and in that sense it's a very lightweight framework, and it speaks to what need to be produced to represent an enterprise's architecture and stops there. Architecture practitioners often find it useful to have more detailed definitions, standards, and guidance covering topics such as the methodology, which provides guidance on what process to follow, the capabilities and skills that need to be in place to run an enterprise architecture practice, and so forth, hence to provide an example of a framework that offers all of these and much more. We will now go through TOGAF framework. TOGAF stands for The Open Group Architecture Framework, and it is developed by The Open Group, which is a vendor and technology neutral industry consortium which over 400 member organizations. The framework has been enhanced periodically since its inception in the early 90s. The current version as of this recording is version 9. 1.

TOGAF 9.1 Specified in Six Parts

- Architecture Content Framework
- The Architecture Development Method (ADM)
- ADM Guidelines and Techniques
- The Enterprise Continuum
- The Architecture Capabilities Framework
- The TOGAF Reference Models

The framework is specified in six major parts comprising Architecture Content Framework, the Architecture Development Method, the ADM Guidelines and Techniques, Enterprise Continuum, The Architecture Capabilities Framework, the TOGAF Reference Models.

Architecture Content Framework

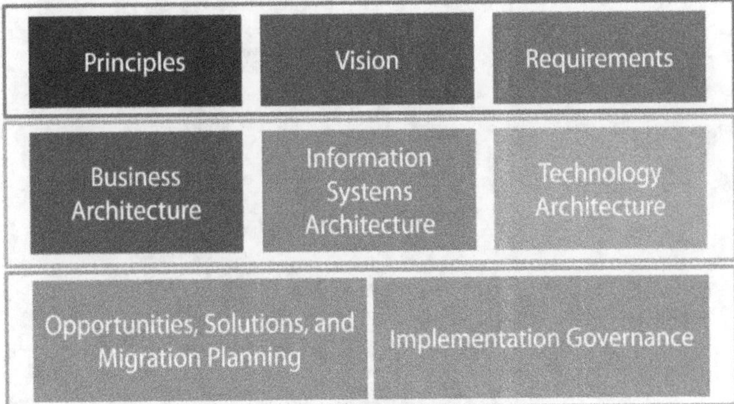

- TOGAF content framework provides a more prescriptive metamodel describing the kinds of building blocks
- A building block (described using catalogues, matrices, diagrams, patterns etc.) represents an architectural or solution component that can be reused
- A collection of building blocks is referred to as architecture artefact

The content framework in TOGAF provides a more prescriptive metamodel as compared to Zachman Framework, and it defines the kinds of building blocks that may be used to describe an enterprise architecture and their interrelationships. A building block represents an architectural or solution component that can be potentially reused. Building blocks are described using catalogs, matrices, diagrams, patterns, et cetera, which are collectively referred to as architectural artifacts.

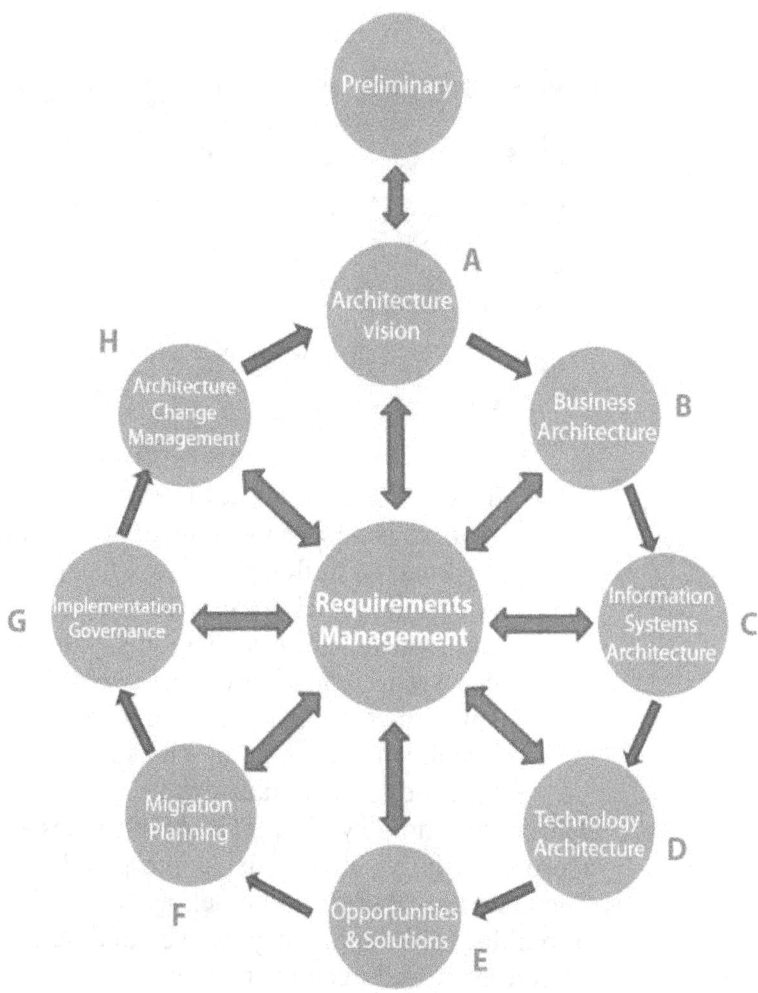

TOGAF Architecture Development Method (ADM)

- ADM is the core of the TOGAF framework
- It essentially describes the sequence of inter-related steps which constitutes an iterative process for developing enterprise architecture
- The framework does not prescribe the number of iterations or the scope of each iteration

- This iterative process can be adapted to the context of each organization
- The framework explicitly encourages tailoring the ADM for effectiveness in the context of a given enterprise

Unlike the Zachman Framework, which only provides the content metamodel and does not prescribe a methodology, the TOGAF content framework is intended to be used alongside the TOGAF ADM, or the Architecture Development Method, which is the process model of TOGAF. The Architecture Development Method is at the core of the TOGAF framework and essentially describes the sequence of interrelated steps which constitutes an iterative process. The iterative process can be adapted to the context of each organization to produce a business aligned and organization-specific architecture process for describing its enterprise architecture. Although the framework talks about an iterative style of architecture development, it does not comment on the number of iterations or

scope of work for each iteration; hence, the breadth and depth of coverage in each iteration can be data mined by each organization to meet its specific needs. Also, the operational aspects of the iterative process such as, for example, would there be any mandatory checkpoints, how many teams will work across iterations and faces, how the team cycle between phases, et cetera, are not prescribed and hence can be tailored to meet the organization's needs.

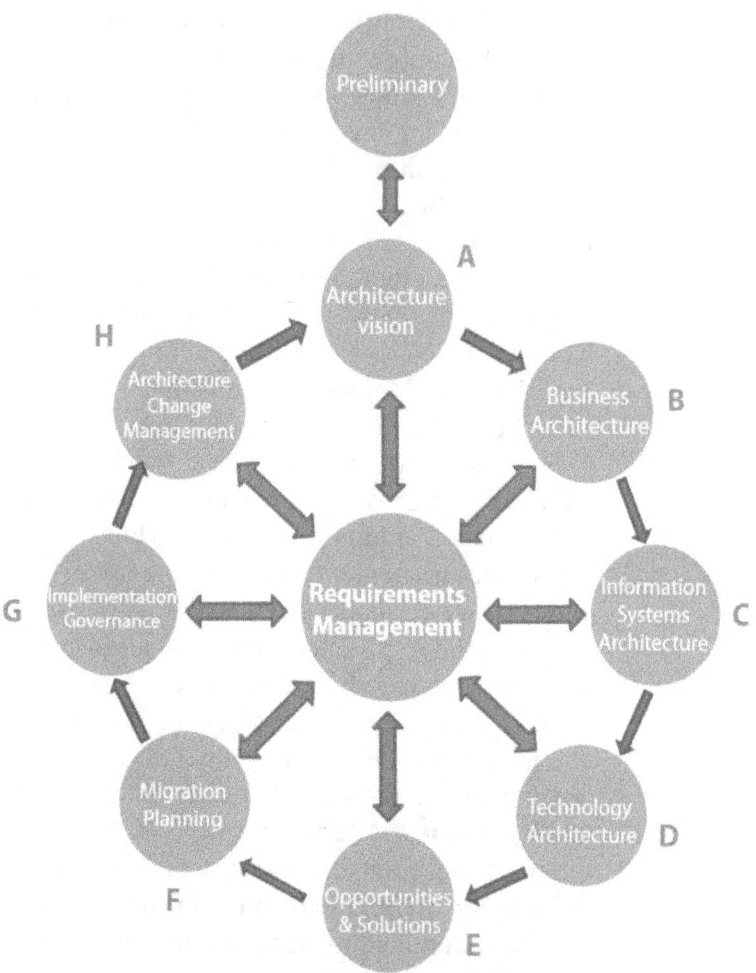

- Preliminary Phase : Customizing the framework to organizational context Necessary approvals and funding activities required to support the architecture work Determining the governing principles
- Phase A: The architectural vision is established Scope of iteration is defined Stakeholders are identified
- Phase B: Business architecture is developed in alignment with architecture vision

- Phase C: Information systems architecture, incorporating both Applications architecture Information (Data) architecture
- Phase D: Captures and describes the building blocks that make up the enterprise's technology infrastructure
- Phase E: Identifies how the developed architecture can be delivered and realized through solutions
- Phase F: Formulates an architecture road map that describes transition from current state to future state architecture
- Phase G: Provides the architectural oversight of implementation
- Phase H: Establishes procedures for change management while transitioning from current state to target state
- Requirements Management : Operates through all phases of the ADM. Collaboratively managing architectural requirements. Ensures alignment with vision and iteration scope

In the preliminary phase of TOGAF, most organizations define a customized framework that are tailored to meet their organizational context. In fact, this activity of customizing the framework along with the necessary approvals and funding activities required to support the architectural work and data mining the governing architectural principles are typical activities that happens in the preliminary phase. In Phase A, that is the first phase of the iterative method, the architectural vision is established. The scope of the iteration is defined, and the key stakeholders are identified. This phase is followed by a business architecture phase, which is where the business architecture development occurs in alignment with the architecture vision. Phase C is the information systems architecture phase which influence both the applications architecture and the information or data architecture. Phase D is the technology architecture phase which captures and describes the building blocks that make up the enterprise's technology infrastructure. Phase E is the opportunities and solution phase which identifies how the development architecture can be delivered and realized through solutions developed as part of various enterprise projects, programs, and initiatives. Phase F is the migration planning phase that addresses the formulation of an architecture roadmap that helps transition the enterprise from its current state to a future target state architecture. Phase G is the governance phase which provides the architectural oversight of the implementation. Phase H is the architectural change management phase which establishes procedures for change management while transitioning from current state to target state. Requirements management phase essentially operates through all phases of the ADM, collaboratively managing architectural requirements through interactions with enterprise-wide stakeholders and ensuring that the requirements are in alignment with architectural vision and the scope identified for each iteration.

ADM Guidelines and Techniques

- Offers a large number of EA best practices
- Describes the more practical considerations of using the framework
- For example, it offers guidance on issues such as,

- Different approaches that may be followed for architecture development
- How the iterations maybe tailored
- Which approach is better suited for various business scenarios
- How architecture principles can be developed
- How to incorporate security architecture into the
- ADM iterations
- How to manage service oriented architectures through ADM cycles

The section ADM Guidelines and Techniques essentially provides a large number of enterprise architecture best practices gleaned from across the industry. It goes into more practical aspects of using the framework such as, for example, the different approaches to architecture development, how the iterations may be tailored to meet these different approaches, which approach is better suited for various business scenarios, how architectural principles can be developed, how to incorporate security architecture into ADM iterations, how to manage service oriented architectures through ADM cycles, and so forth.

More on TOGAF

Achieving Reuse
- Enterprise repository gets built out through ADM cycles along the lines of Architecture Content Framework specifications

- Overtime, the architecture repository of the enterprise grows in volume
- It is important for the enterprise to harvest existing building blocks and architectural assets to create new architectures and solutions

While the enterprise architecture teams deliver architectural outcomes through the phases and iterations of the ADM cycle, the enterprise's architecture repository gets built out along the guidelines provided by Architecture Content Framework. Over time, the architecture repository of the enterprise could collect a huge volume of artifacts representing various architectural building blocks, and it is important for the enterprise to be able to harvest existing building blocks and architectural assets to create new architectures and solutions.

- TOGAF framework recommends a view of the architecture repository through what it refers to as the Enterprise Continuum
- Enterprise Continuum is a view of the enterprise's architecture that facilitate discovery, consistent communication and reuse

TOGAF framework recommends a view of the architecture repository, which it refers to as the Enterprise Continuum, in order to facilitate discovery, consistent communication, and reuse of architecture building blocks and artifacts.

Essentially, the Enterprise Continuum is a view of the architecture and solution repository organized in such a manner that the users can traverse the architecture assets ranging from the most generic and foundational architecture reference models through to industry-specific and further to organization-specific architecture models in order to leverage existing assets, rather than expending energy reinventing the metaphorical wheel.

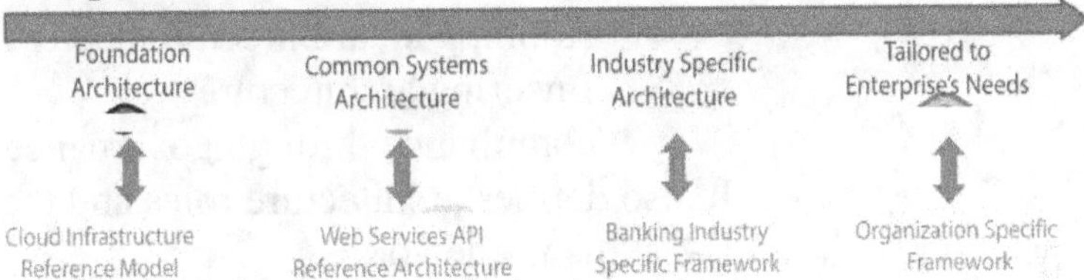

For example, a bank adopting a cloud-centric computing model might use a cloud infrastructure reference model as a foundational reference architecture and look at using, say, a web service's API based architecture as a reference for building out its systems on the cloud infrastructure. It might then identify a backing industry-specific reference architecture, such as BIAN, which stands for Banking Industry Architecture Network, as an industry- specific reference architecture, and then further create its organization-specific architecture by leveraging and customizing these generic architecture models instead of reinventing everything from the scratch. An architect working to solve a specific problem such as, for example, say, a single sign-on architecture, can browse through the continuum of artifacts to look for any precedence, patterns, or best practice guidance that could be leveraged before attempting to solve the problem independently. In order to successfully operate an architecture function within an enterprise, it is necessary to put in place appropriate organization structures, processes, roles and responsibilities and skills to realize

the architecture capability. The Architecture
Capability Framework section of TOGAF
provides guidelines in this area.

- Architecture capability framework
  offers guidelines on
  - Establishing and running an EA
    capability
  - Running an architecture board
  - Ensuring architecture
    compliance through governance
- It also defines architecture roles and the
  EA skills framework
- The guidance in its current form is not
  entirely complete and is expected to be
  further elaborated in future versions of
  the framework

It offers guidelines on establishing the
enterprise architecture capability, establishing
and running an architecture board, ensuring
architecture compliance by incorporating
governance. It also defines architecture roles
and enterprise architecture skills framework.
However, the guidance in its current form is not
entirely complete and is expected to be further
elaborated in future versions of the framework.
In addition to these, TOGAF offers some
generic technical reference models, which is not
updated since the early releases of the
framework, but it is still used as a baseline
reference model by some organizations.

Comparing TOGAF & Zachman Frameworks

- TOGAF is more prescriptive and
  incorporates lot more guidance than
  Zachman framework
- Zachman framework is primarily a
  content metamodel and an enterprise
  architecture ontology
- TOGAF framework integrates six
  different dimensions including a content

- framework, process model, the capabilities framework, a large body of best practices guidelines and techniques, the enterprise continuum and some reference models
- TOGAF ADM allows a lot of flexibility in its iterative process model, while Zachman deliberately does not prescribe a process model
- Some enterprises use Zachman framework for its content metamodel while adopting TOGAF ADM for a process model

That completes the overview of the TOGAF, and if you compare Zachman Framework with TOGAF framework, you will not miss the fact that TOGAF is more prescriptive and elaborate while Zachman Framework is primarily an ontology and metamodel of enterprise architecture. TOGAF integrates six different dimensions which include the content framework, the process model, the capabilities framework, a large body of best practice guidelines and techniques, the enterprise continuum, and the architecture reference models. TOGAF ADM allows a lot of flexibility in its iterative process model while Zachman Framework deliberately does not prescribe a process model. Some enterprises use Zachman Framework for its content metamodel while customizing TOGAF ADM for a process model. In recent times, TOGAF framework seems to be gaining in popularity in large enterprises, both in private and government sectors; however, Zachman, with its simple architecture metamodel, is still popular with many organizations and practitioners. Another key trend in the industry is the increasing adoption of agility, and hence there is an increasing demand on enabling enterprise architecture function in an agile fashion. This aspect of architecture is discussed in more detail in module nine of this book.

Quick Recap

- We began by looking at generic definition of conceptual frameworks before exploring enterprise architecture frameworks
- We then looked at Zachman framework and how it offers a metamodel and ontology that enables defining the enterprise architecture from various stakeholder perspectives
- Finally we looked at TOGAF, which is a more elaborate EA framework incorporating a content framework, process model, capability framework, guidelines and reference models

With that, we come to the end of module two, and to recap we began by looking at generic definition of conceptual frameworks before looking at enterprise architecture frameworks. We then covered Zachman Framework and how it offers a metamodel and ontology that enables defining the enterprise architecture from the perspective of various stakeholders. Finally, we looked at TOGAF, which is a more elaborate enterprise architecture framework incorporating a content framework, process model, capability framework, guidelines, and reference models.

Module:3 Business Architecture

Introduction

Module Focus
- Why Business Architecture?
- Business Architecture Definition
- Methods & Tools Overview

In this module, we will cover business architecture. In this introductory section, we will explore the relevance of business architecture, the problems it addresses, and look at opportunities and value it represents to the business. In a subsequent section, we will look at business architecture's formal definition and understand the implication of that definition. And finally, in the last section we will look at some of the methods and tools used by business architecture to capture the business-centric perspectives. So then, let's get on with it. William Ulrich, in his book Business Architecture, The Art and Practice of Business Transformation, uses a brilliant analogy depicting some scenes from the James Cameron movie Titanic to convey the relevance of business architecture. Let me present the same analogy to convey business architecture's value proposition here. So let's beam ourselves into the thick of the plot. I am referring to the scenes that cover the unfolding of the events just after the iceberg impact. I have here tried to map the sequence of events from the point of impact to the point where captain decides to take a decisive book of action. So the iceberg impact occurs. A handful of people actually witness the impact as it happens. Most passengers felt the impact and knew something happened, but they looked around, and it didn't look too bad, and chose to carry on as if it is business as usual. Some crew members who had direct knowledge of the impact, including the captain, know that it could be potentially serious, but no one is sure of the extent of the damage. Shortly after the impact, you can see the architect, or the chief designer of the ship, Thomas Andrews, played by actor Victor Garber, pacing down the passageway with scrolls of drawings tucked under his arm, and shortly afterwards that is the scene of the meeting between the architects and other senior crew members. Here the architect describes where the ship is impacted, and he is able to logically then analyze and predict the consequence of the impact. He reveals the bad news to the men around him, and he is able to predict how long the ship can hold up. He probably might have been able to identify what could be done to delay the inevitable. And rewind just a few minutes back, and it is a scene of utter confusion. The captain and crew were just as confused and clueless as everyone else around them on what is about to eventuate, and therefore lacked a clear book of action to move forward. After the meeting though, the architect's knowledge on how the ship is built and his ability to arrive at a logical prognosis of what might eventuate

next empowers the captain with sufficient insights to make some good decisions and therefore take the right book of actions. And we know from the movie, as well as from documented historic facts, that these actions by the captain and the crew led to many hundreds of lives being saved. To tie the analogy back to our context, an enterprise is like a large ship and is operated by people who understand how to operate and navigate it, but don't necessarily understand how it is put together. Business architecture and business architects fulfill the role similar to the architect in our analogy by creating and maintaining multiple perspectives and viewpoints of the enterprise that hold the insight and understanding of how everything hangs together.

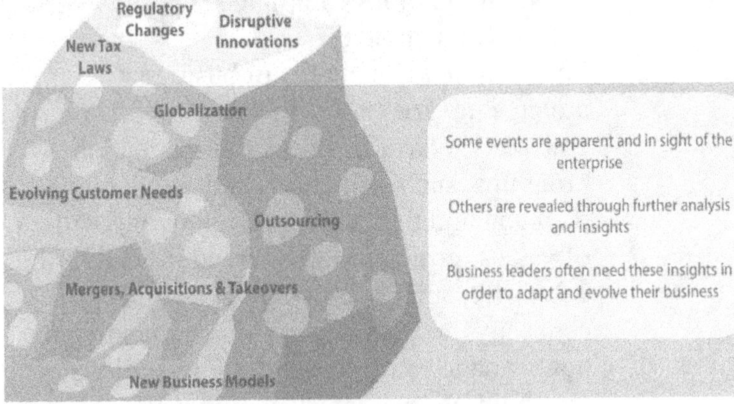

Businesses regularly encounter iceberg events in the book of its operation, and business leaders often need the insights and knowledge of how their enterprise will be impacted by these events and the actions they need to take to adapt and emerge successful when it uncovers an opportunity or where it faces a problem or crisis.

- Business architecture is an important tool for business leaders
- It brings a purely business perspective
- Informs all other architecture domains

Business architecture as a competency is an important tool in the arsenal of a business leader to obtain the clarity and insights necessary to help them decide the next book of action. Business architecture also brings in purely business perspective of the enterprise to enterprise architecture, which then informs all other architectural domains.

Transformation Scenarios

- Rolling out strategic changes
- Mergers and acquisitions
- Aligning to a new set of values
- New products/ services
- Globalization
- Operational streamlining
- Regulatory compliance
- Outsourcing

Some of the key benefits of business architecture are realized when enterprise embarks on large business transformation programs, such as mergers and acquisitions, planning and their rollout. Rolling out new set of values, principles, and directions across the enterprise, such as moving to customer-centricity, new product rollout, expanding to newer market or globalization, operational streamlining, regulatory compliance management, analyzing outsourcing options, etc.

Formal Definition of Business Architecture

In this section, we will define business architecture formally and examine this definition to understand the discipline in more detail.

Business architecture

- Business architecture is the blueprint of the enterprise that provides a common understanding of the organization, and is used to align strategic objectives to tactical demands.

Business Architecture Working Group defines business architecture as follows. Business architecture is the blueprint of the enterprise that provides a common understanding of the organization, and it is used to align strategic objectives to tactical demands. Let's investigate this definition a bit.

Three Components of The Definition

- The blueprint
- Common understanding of the organization
- Aligning strategic objectives to tactical demands

The definition can be broken into three main components represented by the following phrases, the blueprint, common or shared understanding of the organization, aligning strategic objectives to tactical demands.

Blueprint of the Enterprise

- Blueprint implies design or a specification that shows how things are or can be put together to deliver an intended outcome

A blueprint implies design or specification that shows how things are put together or can be put together to deliver an outcome. To use an analogy, if you have come across ready-to-assemble furniture, the ones that arrive in a flat pack and requires you to assemble them following a few diagrams and a short set of instructions supported by an inventory list of materials which come in the pack, well these instructions and inventory lists, etc. in a sense is what business architecture provides for business. It represents the know-how of how business is put together.

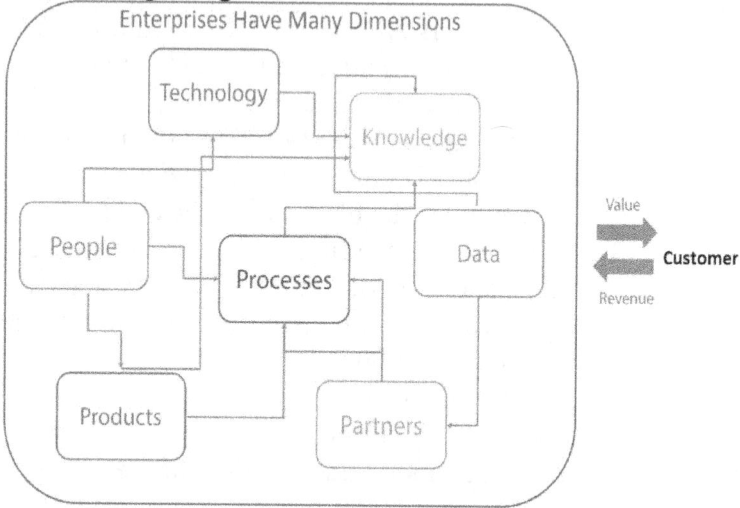

Enterprises have many dimensions, the people, process, technology, products and services, capabilities, customers, and so forth. Business architecture, through various artifacts, provide an understanding of how these dimensions come together within the enterprise in order to deliver value to customers and in turn generate revenue for the business.

Common Understanding of the Enterprise

- 80 - 90% of the employees don't understand the enterprise's vision and strategic objectives
- Business architecture enables key decision makers at all levels to operate based on a shared understanding of the enterprise

Common and shared understanding of business. It is a common observation in many studies that across various industries about 80% to 90% of the employees of the organization do not understand the enterprise's mission, strategic objectives, and how these objectives relate to what they are doing on a day- to-day basis.

Business architecture by definition attempts to address this gap to enable key decision makers at all levels to have a shared understanding of the goals of the organization as a whole in order that they make effective

decisions and choices in alignment with strategic intent and objectives.

Business Operate in a Dynamic Business Environment

It is important to note that the businesses today and in the emerging future are operating in a dynamic business environment. What we mean by environment in this case is the sum total of external forces with which the enterprise would have to negotiate and adapt to in order to sustain and grow its business. Changes can come at different rates and are often unpredictable, and businesses need a blueprint that informs executives and key decision makers what the implications of these changes may be before actually rolling out those changes. It is also important to note that with each change the business architecture evolves and needs to be kept up-to-date.

- Business Architecture is a dynamic blueprint of the enterprise

- And it represents a common (shared) understanding of the enterprise

Hence, it would appropriate to say that the business architecture is a dynamic blueprint of the enterprise that evolves to remain current and represent a shared understanding of the enterprise. Aligning Strategic Objectives to Tactical Demands. The whole intent here seems to be to seek alignment between strategic objectives and tactical demands. As it happens, enterprises typically lack the luxury to reboot or start afresh at will, which could have afforded the flexibility to build out the ideal state, process, structures, and capabilities from scratch. It, however, needs to implement its strategies from where it finds itself currently, and this often means that there are serious operational and tactical demands that contend with strategic priorities. Enterprises often find themselves lost for direction without a clear framework that helps decision makers to make effective choices and tradeoffs between strategic and tactical demands. This gap is again addressed by business architecture through a combination of artifacts, such as business architecture road map, strategy map, initiative maps, balance scorecards, etc. That brings us to the end of this section, and in the next section, which will be the final section of this module, we will uncover what form business architecture actually takes in the real world, that is what typical artifacts are produced, and what perspectives and viewpoints they offer.

Capability and Value Maps

If you want to examine and understand a certain terrain, one of the best tools to turn to is a map. We all know maps are of different kinds, and each of them reveal different kinds of information about the terrain. For example, you can have physical maps, political maps, climatic maps, maps depicting roads, rails, and other transport networks, and so forth. Depending on what information you need and how you want to work with the terrain, you would choose an appropriate kind of map that provides this information, or you might choose to use a combination of them. Business architecture uses a similar approach to comprehending the enterprise. In this section, we will be looking at various tools that are employed in the business architecture to comprehend the enterprise from various perspectives.

Business Architecture Maps

- Capability Maps
- Value Maps
- Information Maps
- Organization Maps
- Strategy Maps
- Initiative Maps
- Stakeholder Maps

Capability Maps, Value Maps, Information Maps & Organization Maps are four legs of business architecture blueprint

Specifically, we will be looking at the following four foundational maps: capability maps, value maps, information maps, and organization maps. Together they are referred to as the four legs of the business architecture blueprint as they represent the stable baseline set of artifacts that describes the enterprise from the business perspective. They can be used as the foundation for further analysis to derive other maps, such as strategy maps, initiative maps, stakeholder maps, etc. So let's try and understand these tools in more detail. We'll begin with capability maps.

Capability

- Capability signifies a capacity that an enterprise possesses
- They represent the basic building blocks of an enterprise
- Capability map captures the enterprise building blocks which forms the vocabulary or "nouns" used across all artefacts of business architecture blueprint

A capability signifies specific ability or capacity that an enterprise possesses to do something. In other words, they represent the basic building blocks of an enterprise when viewed from the perspective of what the enterprise actually does. Capability map attempts to capture and describe the enterprise in terms of building blocks of what it does without going into the details of why and how things get done. The capability building blocks represent the vocabulary or nouns that can be reused by all of the business architecture artifacts. The capability map usually is represented in multiple levels ranging from level one to level six.

Capability Map Level 1 to 3

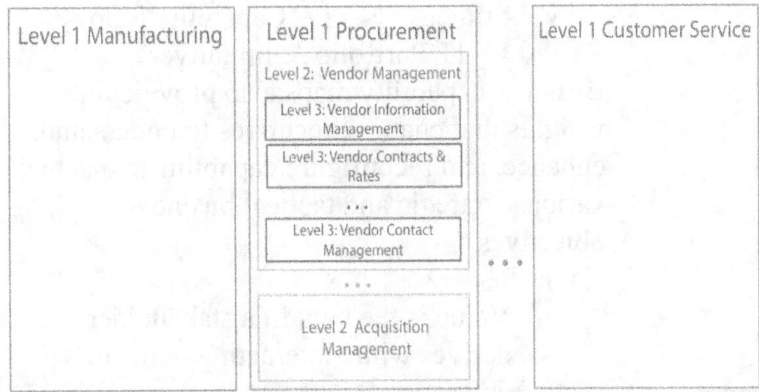

Level one to level three represent higher level abstractions of capabilities, and hence are appropriate to be used in the context of strategy formulation and strategy planning.

Capability Map Level 4 to 6

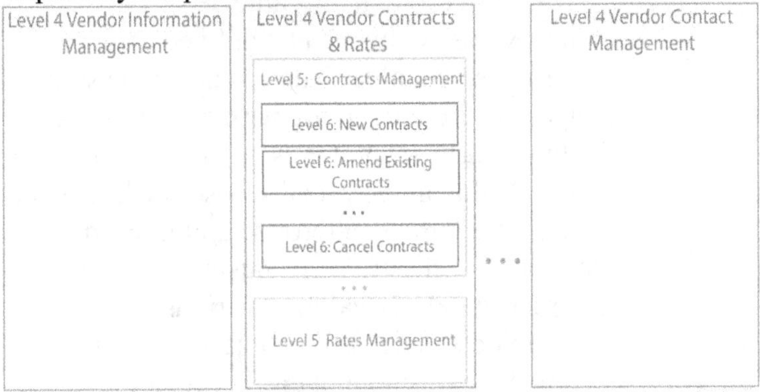

However, level four to level six are more granular, and hence are used for detailed business-to-IT alignment mapping exercises. Capability maps are often used to translate strategic objectives into specific actionable initiatives within capabilities. Therefore, capability maps often serve as a means for translating enterprise vision and strategic objectives into specific IT initiatives, that is projects and programs of work. For this reason, capability maps are referred to as Rosetta Stone of enabling business IT alignment.

Rosetta Stone of Business IT Alignment

- Strategy <<-->> Capability Map <<-->> IT Portfolio & Initiatives

Business capability maps also provide the insights that enable executives to understand, enhance, and reconfigure capabilities to achieve various strategic and tactical business objectives.

Value

- Value is the benefit a stakeholder derives while interacting with an enterprise
- Value maps visually describe how value gets created in the enterprise
- Value maps describe how an enterprise orchestrates its business capabilities in order to deliver value

Value Maps. Value can be defined as the benefit a stakeholder, such as an end customer, derives while interacting with an enterprise. Value is fundamental reason why an enterprises exists. Value maps visually describe how value gets created in the enterprise and how an enterprise orchestrates its business capabilities in order to deliver value to various stakeholders, such as customers, partners, suppliers, etc. Value maps, hence, are not standalone entities. They make use of capability maps, and it is an important artifact that is utilized to study, understand, and enhance the effectiveness and efficiency of enterprise processes.

Types of Value Maps

- Value Chains
- Value Streams
- Value Networks

Value maps can be of three types, value chains, value streams, and value networks.

Value Chains

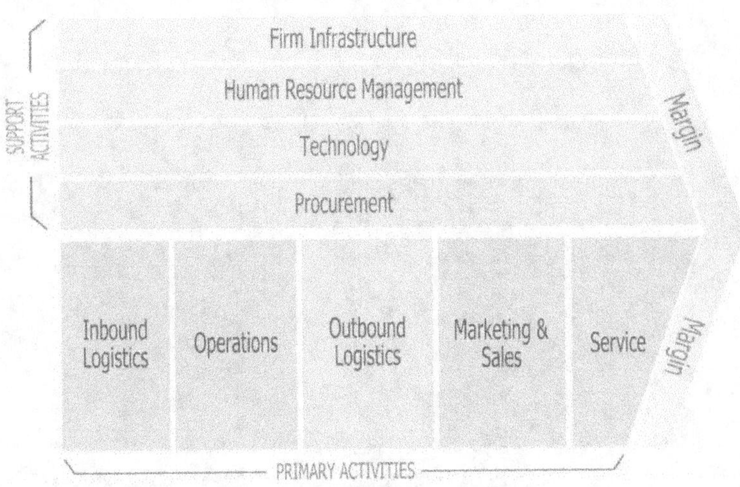

Value chains are the oldest of the value mapping technique introduced in the 1980's by Michael Porter of Harvard Business School. The method focused on identifying and distinguishing between value-adding processes and supporting processes within the enterprise. This method of value mapping focuses its analysis based on generic pattern of five core activities, namely inbound logistics, operations, outbound logistics, marketing, and sales and service. This kind of mapping used to be generically applicable to most product companies in manufacturing industry sectors, but it's not always relevant or suitable in the information and knowledge-based industries.

Value Stream. Value streams attempts to address the limitations of value chain, especially for industries which struggled with the value chains. By definition, value stream is the end-to-end collection of activities that create a result for the customer who may be the ultimate end customer or an internal end user. Value stream is therefore a more generic approach to performing value analysis than value chains. Both value chains and value streams represent the linear chain of activities leading to value delivery to a stakeholder. However, in many instances the relationship among stakeholders is not linear, but a complex web and requires non-linear representation to capture these complex interrelationships. Value networks enable capturing these relationships. Value Networks

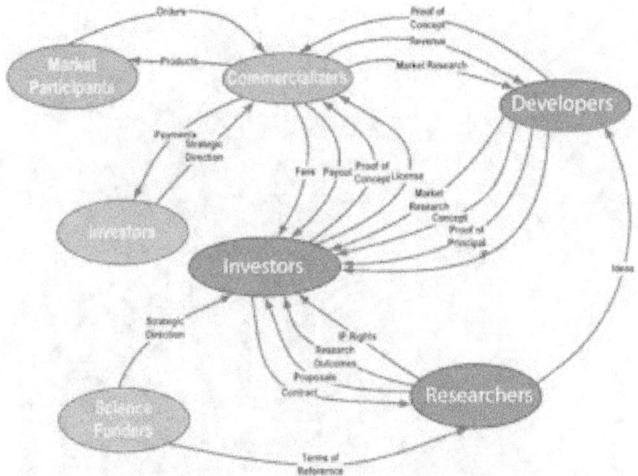

- Value networks help capture the complex web of non-linear relationships
- Value networks can be internal focussed or external focussed
- Used by innovators and disruptors to extract greater efficiency and value

Value networks can be created to comprehend the enterprise's internal value networks, or it can have an external focus to understand the dynamics between upstream suppliers and customers, all of the intermediaries, stakeholders, and other entities that may be relevant.

Value maps are used by innovators and disruptors in the quest to simplify and to squeeze out greater efficiencies and higher value.

Information and Organization Maps

Information Maps
- Information Pyramid

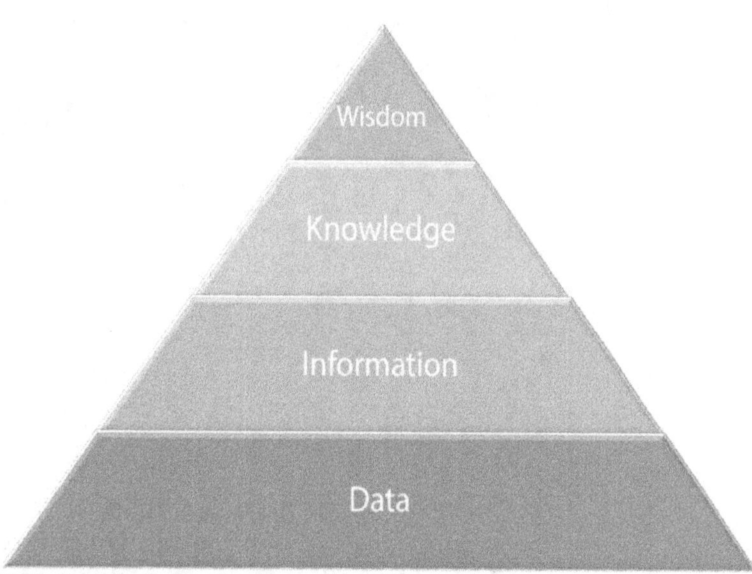

Information maps are a collection of information concepts that are required to manage a business. Let's take a detour to understand information concepts and the idea of an information pyramid, which represents levels of intelligence enabled by data within the enterprise. While data is defined as discrete organized or unorganized collection of objective facts and observations and usually devoid of context, they therefore do not datically lend itself to sense making. They, however, form the raw materials for constructing higher orders of intelligence represented by the information pyramid. Information layer within the pyramid represents processed data, which allows it to be interpreted meaningfully in the light of a certain context. Knowledge, on the other hand, represents the ability to solve problems or create value by applying information. Wisdom can be defined as the higher order of knowledge gleaned from patterns learned by applying knowledge to various kinds of problems or opportunities. The greater the ability to convert objective facts and observations sourced within and outside the organization to information, knowledge, and wisdom, the greater the intelligence of the enterprise, and it impacts its ability to make more informed choices and decisions at all levels. While knowledge and wisdom have a tinge of subjectivity associated with it, as there is a level of judgment involved, and data are too raw and devoid of context, information has the right level of granularity and objectivity that enables stakeholders to communicate using a shared vocabulary in relation to concepts that are key to running the enterprise. These form the information concepts,

Information Concepts

- Encapsulate how the enterprise collectively thinks about what it does
- Along with capabilities they represent the vocabulary for collaborative analysis of the enterprise

and the information concepts encapsulates how the enterprise collectively thinks about what it does, and hence, along with the capabilities, represent the common language that enables collaborative analysis of the business.

Information Map

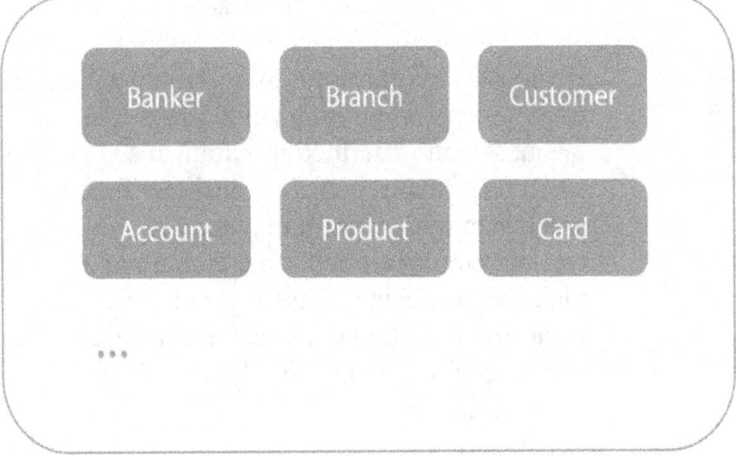

- Arrived by examining capability maps along value streams

Information map takes the form of simple block diagrams representing key information concepts relevant to the enterprise. It is usually arrived at by investigating the capability maps overlaid with value maps in order to keep the focus on specific information that leads to value generation.

Organization Maps

- Organization to Capability Maps
  - Capabilities
  - Business Units

The organization map informs us of internal business units and third parties that actually hold various capabilities and how they participate in value-producing activities. While capabilities and value streams represents the enterprise at a conceptual level of abstraction, the organization map shines the light on how these capabilities are realized within the enterprise.

- Organization maps are composed of business units
- Business units are a logical segment of an enterprise representing a function
- Business units are headed by senior business managers

Business units forms an important idea that are used to construct organization maps where a business unit is defined as a logical segment of a company that represent a business function and hence finds a definite place in an organization chart under the domain of a manager. A business unit is typically a department or division which has a certain accountability, such as marketing, finance, accounting, etc.

Organization

- A social unit of people, systematically structured and managed to meet a need or to pursue collective goals on a continuing basis

An organization can be defined as a social unit of people systematically structured and managed to meet a need or to pursue collective goals on a continual basis. As you can see, the definition is devoid of constraints of corporate boundaries as many third-party entities outside the corporate boundaries typically play a significant role to enable many value streams of the enterprise. Based on this definition of the organization, the organization map therefore holds

not only the information about business units, but provide organization-oriented relationships, including external parties.

Foundational Maps

- Capability Maps
- Value Maps
- Information Maps
- Organization Maps

The four maps discussed so far form the stable and foundational business architecture views of an enterprise and provide the baseline from which further analysis can be done and more views can be created for specific purposes.

Strategy, Initiative, and Stakeholder Maps

Strategy Maps

- idea -->> plan -->> action

Strategy

- Strategy is a high level plan that drives enterprise make its choices and decisions
- Strategy also drives other more detailed plans
- Strategy maps make strategy actionable

We will now quickly cover some of the other commonly used business architecture views that are created from the foundational views. We will begin with strategy map. Strategy, in the context of an enterprise, can be thought of as a high-level plan that an enterprise formulates, which then drives many top-level choices and decisions. The strategy also drives more detail-oriented plans to help align tactical and operational decisions to strategic intent. While strategy conveys the enterprise's intent and helps drive change across the enterprise, business architecture through strategy maps makes strategy actionable.

SWOT Analysis

Strength | Weakness

Opportunity | Threat

Porter's Five Forces Model

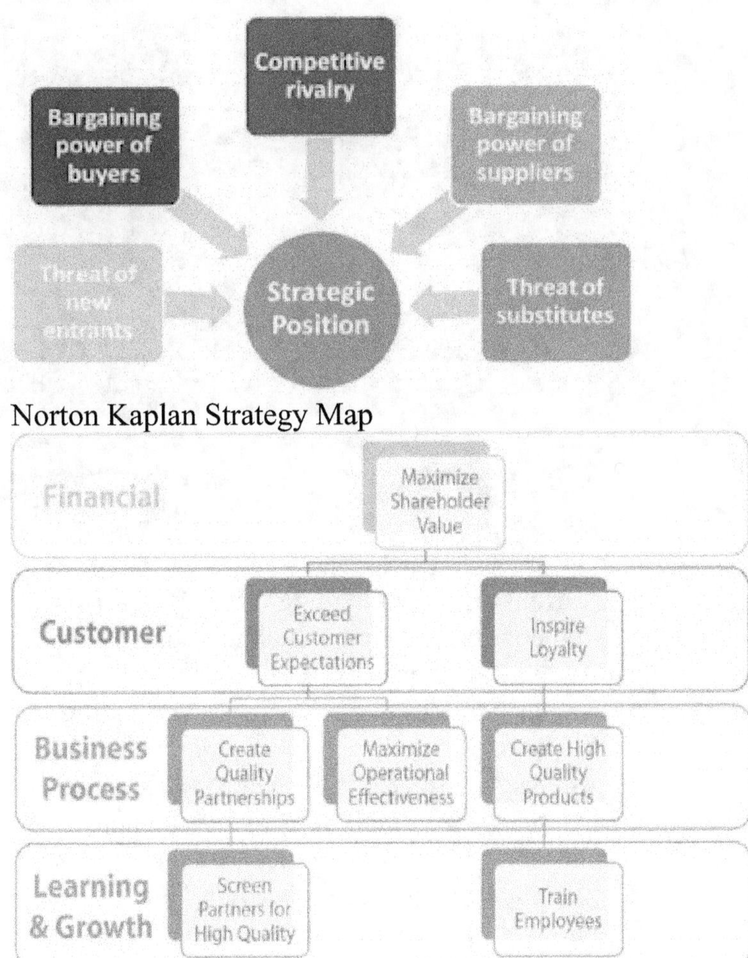

Norton Kaplan Strategy Map

Business Motivation Model

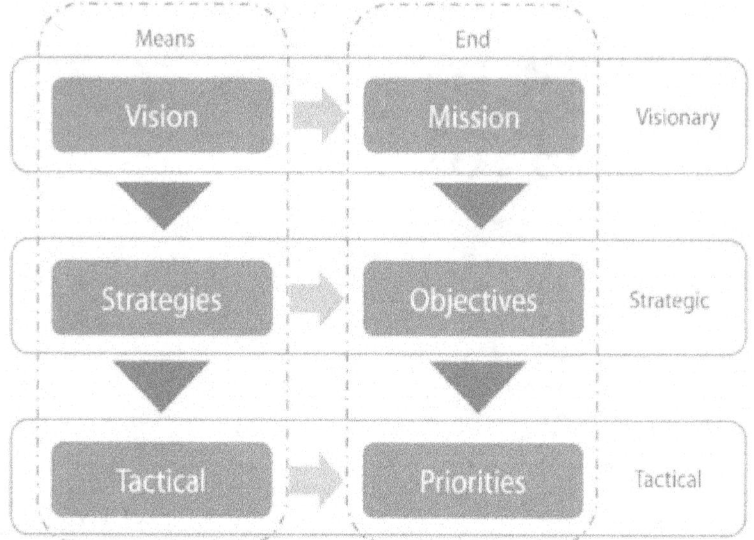

Various strategy mapping techniques are used in the industry today, which includes SWOT Analysis, Porter's Five Forces Model, Norton Kaplan Strategy Map, Business Motivation Map, etc. While the first two, that is the SWOT Analysis and Porter's Five Forces Model assist in strategy formulation by analyzing and classifying forces operating on the enterprise, the other two assist in identifying the implications of strategic objectives and how these objectives interact among each of them and therefore identify what actions and initiatives are required.

Initiative Maps

Various Approaches to Initiative Mapping

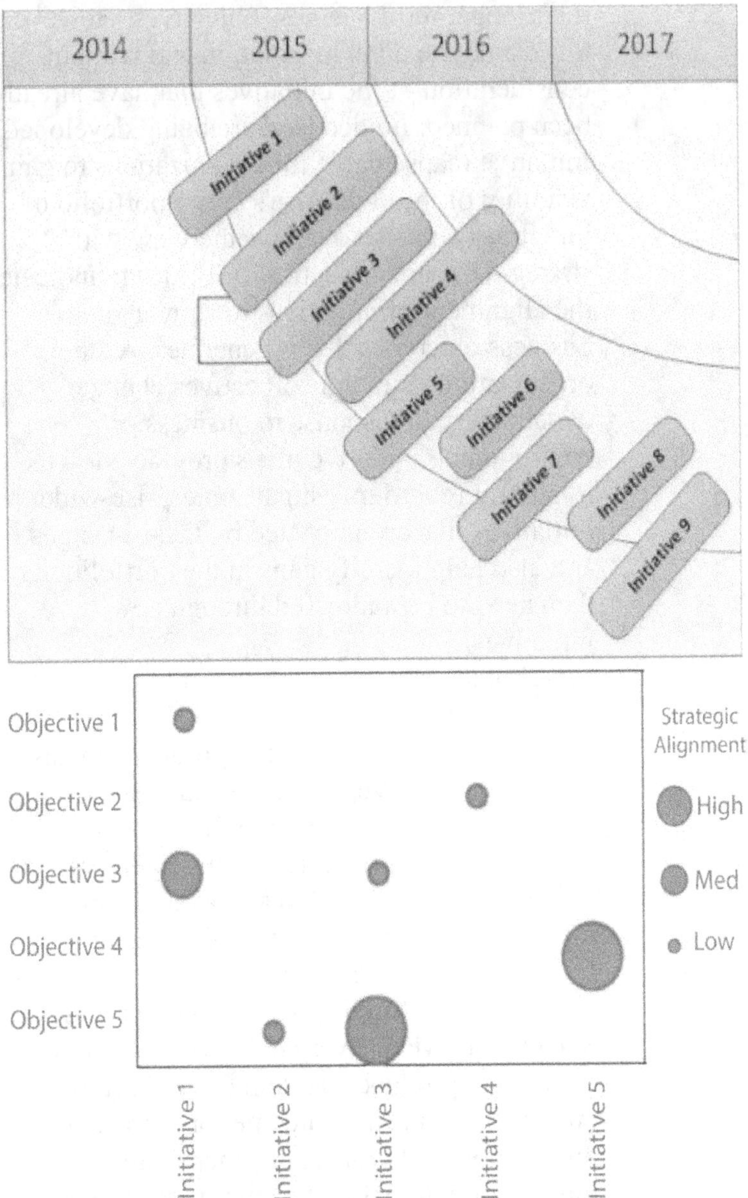

Initiative Maps. To adapt and thrive in the fast-paced business environment, enterprises frequently need to reconcile their strategic intents with the tactical and operational demands and arrive at a portfolio of actionable initiatives to meet their short-term goals and their longer term business objectives. However, this cannot be done in isolation and without consideration of the initiatives that have already been planned, funded, and are being developed. Initiative maps enable the organizations to gain visibility of the enterprise's entire portfolio of initiatives and also overlays the view with strategic intent and tactical priorities to indicate the alignment of initiatives to strategy and business outcomes that it generates. As the organization's strategic objectives change dynamically in response to business environment, initiative maps provide an important tool to investigate enterprise-wide initiatives that are impacted by these changes and also help identify gaps in the portfolio that then need to be addressed through new initiatives.

Stakeholder Map

- Stakeholder
    - Individuals or groups who have a vested interested in the outcomes and the value an enterprise initiative generates are referred to as stakeholders
    - Examples include: Customers, Partners, Suppliers, Distributors, Employees, Regulatory body etc.

Stakeholder Map. Every enterprise initiative is directed to produce a certain desired set of outcomes, and these outcomes are directed at one or more individuals or groups, either internal or external to the enterprise. These individuals or groups who have vested interest in the outcomes and the value generated by the enterprise are referred to as stakeholders. Some examples of stakeholders include customers, partners, suppliers, distributors, employees, regulatory bodies, etc.

Stakeholder mapping is typically used to understand how a stakeholder is triggering or is participating within the value stream.
Stakeholder Mapping

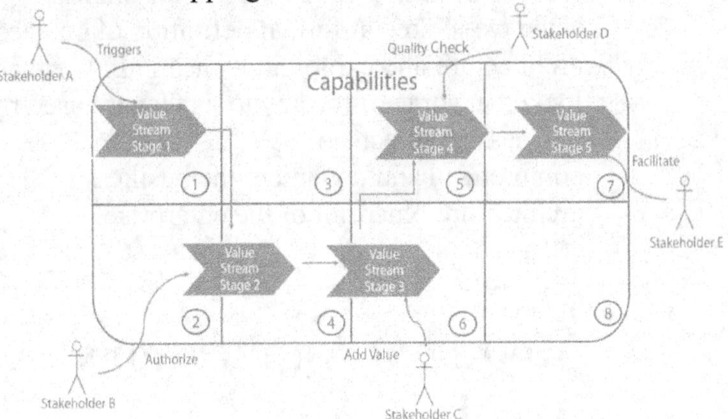

- Mapping stakeholders to initiatives
- Mapping stakeholders to strategy
- Mapping stakeholders to capabilities

However, such mapping can also be done in relation to other views of business architecture as well, for example, mapping stakeholders to initiatives, mapping stakeholders to strategy and the component of the strategy that the stakeholder has ownership of, mapping stakeholders to capabilities that they own or enable. That brings us to the end of the quick overview of some of the key tools used by business architecture for documenting the blueprint, and it also brings us to the end of the current module. And following is a quick summary of what we covered.
Module Summary

- Business Architecture Relevance & Value
- Formal Definition of Business Architecture
- Overview Methods & Tools

In the introductory section, we established the relevance and value of business architecture and some of the key transformation scenarios where business architecture's value shines.
Then we looked at formal definition of business architecture and explored its meaning. We then looked at some of the key tools that are used by business architects to
comprehend and document the business architecture blueprint of the enterprise.

Module:4 Applications Architecture

Introduction

The current module will focus on applications architecture. Applications architecture represent the architecture of the entire portfolio of enterprise business applications and not so much on how an individual application is architected.
Applications Architecture emphasizes on:
- Taking strategic view of enterprise applications
- Creating evolving standards
- Creating policies and guidelines
- Applications architectures inform and guide:
    - Procurement
    - Development
    - Integration
    - Deployment

- Delivery

Hence, the emphasis is on taking a strategic view on the enterprise applications and to create evolving standards, policies, and guidelines that inform and guide the procurement, development, integration, deployment, and delivery of enterprise applications. In this module, we will explore applications architecture along the following lines.

Module Focus

- Why Applications Architecture?
- Foundational Concepts & Context
- Future Directions & Trends

First, we will look at why applications architecture is important. Then we will look at some of the foundational concepts of applications architecture, how applications architecture fits into the larger scheme of enterprise architecture. And finally, we will look at the future directions and trends into space.

Why Applications Architecture?

So let's begin by exploring why applications architecture is important for an enterprise. Software has increasingly taken center stage in most enterprises. Over the last several decades driven by the need to remain competitive with their product and service offerings in the marketplace, or to achieve greater efficiency through automation, or to gain greater insights into various facets of the organization's functioning, businesses across all industry sectors have invested heavily in business applications. Today, most modern enterprises depend on software to run all of their core

business processes, their customer-facing channels, their vendor and partner integrations, as well as more recently in establishing and expanding their active social presence, branding, and cloud through social media channels. We are indeed living through a time where every business is quite literally a software business irrespective of its industry, the products, services, or the value they produce for the end consumer. Business applications can be seen as the software instantiation of the enterprise's business capabilities. In the new and emerging business landscape driven by employed end consumers and fast moving start-ups who constantly innovate their products, services, and business model, there are no easy means of sustaining competitive advantage other than through anticipating and responding to change continuously and through continuous business innovation. An enterprise's applications architecture, which is architecture of the entire portfolio of business applications taken as a whole will be a key determinant of how quickly and effectively the business as a whole can evolve by
responding to the challenges thrown at it and the opportunities it uncovers.
Case Study – Large Financial Services Organization

- Regulatory changes to protect endconsumers obtaining financial advice
- The regulation mandated compliance by a hard end date
- Resulted in large number of application to be modified
- An effective and flexible applications architecture could have accomplished this at a fraction of the cost

For instance, a large, well-established financial services enterprise that I consulted for in the past found itself at the receiving end of some regulatory changes that came into effect to protect the interest of end consumers obtaining financial advice. The regulation mandated complaints by a hard end date. Given the state of the applications architecture prevalent in the enterprise, enabling these regulatory changes first of all meant changing a large number of systems that the enterprise used to conduct and record its customer interactions. Although some backend interfaces were expected to be modified to accommodate these changes, many changes were required in the downstream and parallel system due to unanticipated ripple effects. A well-architected portfolio of applications and services could have potentially enabled the organization to comply with the regulation at a fraction of the cost. This particular enterprise had to allocate a significantly large outlay of investment to enable these sweeping changes within the stipulated timeframe with no significant competitive benefits or return on investments on offer.

Case Study – Online Retail Organization

- Expected to complete a customer centric redesign in 12 to 18 months
- The challenge of integrating more than 120 of its backend systems proved too much
- Development eventually completed in 5 years
- Overtaken by nimbler and faster moving competition

Another client that sought to revamp its online services to better align with its customer needs, in the initial analysis expected to complete the

entire initiator within 12 to 18 months.
However, the complicated changes involved in integrating more than 120 of its core systems running on disparate platforms through a newly created

service- oriented architecture layer only revealed itself progressively as the project rolled on through a heavily _____ process. In the end, the revamped application saw the light of day after five long years of development, and by that timeframe the opportunity window to present a differentiated and compelling customer experience had all but dried out in the wake of faster moving and more nimble competition.

- Overall architecture of the applications portfolio
- Consciously and continuously crafted and evolved principles, practices, policies and tools to realize an effective applications architecture can give it a huge competitive edge

In such cases as these, the overall architecture of the applications portfolio and how well the enterprise consciously and continuously crafted and evolved principles, practices, policies, and tools to realize such an architecture in parallel with its evolving business needs can be a great help to achieve its business objectives efficiently. Following now some of the examples of scenarios where the value and impact of applications architecture becomes readily apparent.

Scenarios

- Mergers & Acquisitions
- Business Operating Model
- Compliance Management
- Vendor Management
- Risk Management

Mergers & Acquisitions. Applications architecture may be used in pre and post merger and acquisitions situations. Pre-merger analysis of the architecture can be used to produce strategic fitment assessment and to get an understanding of the cost outlay involved in integrating applications and systems. An applications architecture can be used to analyze and understand post-merger consolidation initiatives. Business Operating Model. Applications architecture can provide insights into the gaps or redundancies in the current application portfolio and enhance an organization's ability to consolidate and streamline its processes and improve overall effectiveness. Compliance Management. Applications architecture allows the organization to look at its systems from a compliance perspective and direct application investments across the portfolio to enable greater transparency. Vendor Management. The holistic view of application inventory provided by applications architecture arms management for vendor negotiations and gives the organization an opportunity to lower license and maintenance cost by consolidating vendors. Risk Management. It is critical to know what the riskiest business and technical issues are across the entire applications portfolio so that the economic, reputational, and other implications for the business can be understood and leads to prioritization of these issues and thereby help in the planning of planning of remedial measures. Hence, clearly there is a need for organizations to take a strategic view of its enterprise's applications portfolio and architect them for interoperability, flexibility, and rapid evolution as the enterprise meanders through the rapidly changing business landscape.

Foundational Concepts and Context

So what exactly what do we mean by taking a strategic view of the applications portfolio, and where does applications architecture fit in the overall scheme? Well, to get a high-level picture, let's look briefly at TOGAF architecture development method.

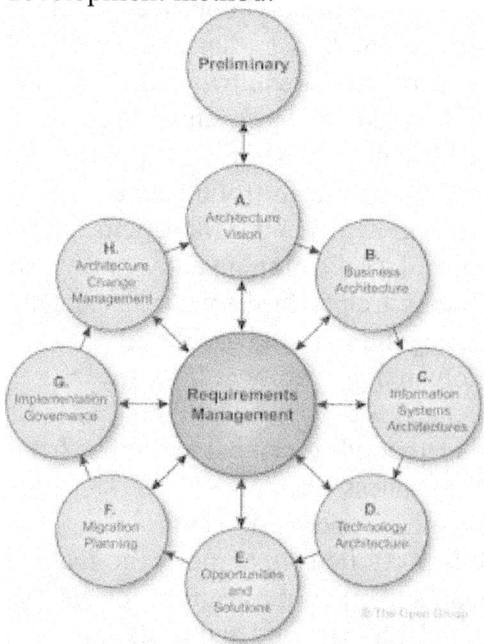

As described earlier in module two, the step C of the architecture development method, which is the information systems architecture, represents the stage in the process where applications and data architecture of the enterprise is delivered, and you can observe from the diagram that this state is informed and influenced by business architecture, which in turn is influenced by the architectural vision. This is quite understandable given that enterprise applications realizes and instantiates capabilities and processes within a business, Applications Instantiates Capabilities & Processes

- Key inputs to applications portfolio architecture include:
  - Strategic vision
  - Strategic business objectives
  - List of business capabilities

and hence the enterprise's strategic mission and objectives, an identified list of capabilities, are key inputs into designing an application portfolio for the enterprise.

Influences on Applications Architecture

- Capabilities Based Planning
- Strategic Priorities
- Applications Architecture

In most instances, organizations starting an enterprise architecture practice usually don't get to start on a clean slate, and they typically inherit a legacy applications portfolio of several lines of business applications and point solutions. And hence, most applications architects use business architecture inputs such as capability maps to rationalize their applications portfolio. This involves using capability map and overlaying it with applications that enables these capabilities to create a capability-centric perspective of the applications portfolio.

Applications Portfolio Analysis

- Capability centric view of applications portfolio
- Other architecture perspectives include:
  - Long term strategic objectives

- Operational and tactical priorities
- Business operating model
- Organizational and political structures

Other business architecture perspectives and inputs that are used by applications architects include long-term strategic objectives of the business, it's operational and tactical priorities that would enable keeping the business running, as well as taking advantage of some near-term opportunities. In large enterprises consisting of multiple business units, the priorities of each business unit will need to be factored in and rationalized against the priorities of the enterprise as a whole. The other key considerations also include operating model and how applications and data enable the operating model, which, by the way, is defined as the necessary level of business process integration and standardization for delivering goods and services to customers, the organizational and political structures in order to comprehend the people and human dimensions of the puzzle. Enterprise applications architect creates target state applications portfolio roadmap, taking into consideration:

- Total cost of change
- Return on investments
- Risks and path of least resistance

With these perspectives as their guidance, as well as considering the total cost of change, return on investments, and risks involved, the applications architect determines the target static applications portfolio and create an approach and roadmap for applications portfolio rationalization.

Target State Might Include …

- Identified gaps in application capabilities
- Decision to retire aging and low-value applications
- Modernizing legacy yet high-value applications
- Eliminating redundancy
- Standardizing on common technology platform
- Consolidating applications

This might result in identified gaps in application capabilities, a decision to retire aging and low-value applications, decision to modernize some high-value applications, eliminating redundant applications, standardizing on common technology platform and version, consolidating applications either physically, logically, or both.

Governance and Grooming

- Applications architecture and portfolio rationalization cannot be a one time initiative in today's business environment
- There is a need for continuous grooming and on-going governance
- Applications portfolio architecture management process need to be established
  - Should include executive level sponsorship to enable effective strategic decision making
  - The governance board should include crosscompany business and IT leadership

One of the pitfalls of applications architecture and portfolio rationalization in practice is that it is undertaken as a onetime initiative to set long-term strategic direction with a three to five year horizon in mind with the intention of relisting only at the end of that timeframe. While this approach would have been sufficient for most enterprises few decades ago, today's fast changing business environment in which enterprises operate requires continuous governance and grooming of applications portfolio through establishment of an applications portfolio architecture management process with effective executive-level sponsorship to make the program relevant to the organization and to make strategic decisions. Also, the governance board should include cross-company business and IT leaders in order to provide cross-organizational perspectives, governance, and accountability. That brings us to the end of this section. In the next section, we will explore the current and future trends that are influencing and shaping enterprise applications architecture.

Future Applications Architecture Directions and Trends Overview

"How long would it take for your organization to deploy a change that involves just one single line of code? " Mary Popendieck. Modern hyper-competitive business landscape are driving enterprises to pursue the path of continuous innovation. Business that are able to innovate, experiment, and deliver software-based solutions quickly are outcompeting those that follow more traditional delivery methods. Quarterly cycles that are traditionally used for releasing enterprise software considerably diminishes the amount of experimentation that can be done within an enterprise. This in turn thwarts the enterprise's appetite for radical and systemic innovations required to create competitive differentiation. Enterprises are now increasingly seeking to adopt a new model for creating and releasing software that is more like how web-based businesses such as, for example, Netflix, Instagram, and Twitter does it, as this model allows them to work on several innovation hypotheses and run several experiments to apply to software to production continuously, say about 100 times or more each day as opposed to once in a quarter, and thereby validate and test ideas rapidly and adopt the successful ones while eliminating the unsuccessful ones. This need for continual innovation is driving the adoption of next generation of applications architecture, which is referred to in some quarters at the cloud native application, or born in the cloud applications, mainly because these architectures assume the availability of on-demand provisioning, scaling, and tear down of deployment and remnants.

Modern Business Applications Characteristics

- Fashioned for the cloud
- Support modern user interaction patterns
- Designed to scale elastically
- Optimized to support continuous delivery and/or deployment
- Works within architectural and operational safe guards
- They are antifragile

Some of the characteristics that modern business applications architecture tend to incorporate are as follows. They are fashioned for cloud-based infrastructure. They are architected to support emerging end user interaction patterns. The applications are designed to scale elastically. The architecture practices, processes, and tools are optimized to support continuous delivery and continuous deployment. The applications operate within certain architectural and operational safeguards that are required to support experimentation and risk-taking necessary to innovate. They are antifragile. We will use the remainder of the section to explore each of these characteristics in greater detail.

Cloud Native Apps & Modern End-user Interaction Patterns

One of the key value proposition of modern business applications architecture is its ability to drastically reduce the cycle time and frictions involved in going from concept to cache or mission to value. To enable this, these architectures need rapid provisioning, as well as deprovisioning of the computing environments, as well as the ability to scale them up and down on demand. In other words, these applications architecture approaches does not relate to traditional computing environments based on physical or virtual servers that are individually managed, but rather they are architected to take advantage of private cloud infrastructure such as those enabled through Microsoft Hyper-V Cloud or VMware vSphere-based vCloud suite of technologies. They also cater to the public cloud infrastructure such as those provided by AWS, Microsoft Azure, CSC, IBM SoftLayer, etc. In many instances, these applications straddle both private and public cloud infrastructure. The deployment, management, and configuration of applications that cross multiple amendments are typically handled using automated deployment tools. Some examples of this include Release Management for Visual Studio, or Visual Studio Online from Microsoft, UrbanCode Deploy from IBM, XL Deploy from XebiaLabs, and open source continuous integration tools such as Jenkins. Gartner predicts by 2016 two-thirds of the mobile workforce will own a smart phone, and about 40% of the workforce will be mobile. Businesses today and in the emerging future are under pressure to adopt their business applications rapidly to the changing behaviors and interaction patterns of its end users. Driven by the progressive nature of computing and wireless networks, end users, paid customers, partners, or employees are increasingly expecting business applications to be accessible not only on traditional workstations such as laptops, but they also expect to access these applications on the go on mobile devices such as tablets, smart phones, readables, and other more specialized devices that are relevant to their industry and domain. They expect to have consistent experiences across these platforms and at the same time be able to take advantage of the device form factor, as well as the built-in hardware and platform capabilities offered by the device. An indication of this trend could be seen in platforms such as Netflix, which supports 1, 000+ device types as of February 2015. Developing business applications to support and take advantage of capabilities exposed by multitudes of device types and maintaining consistency and continuity of experience across these present an architectural challenge.

Emergence of API Centric Architecture

- API centric architectures sprung up in response to modern application interaction patterns
- They follow simple design tenets:
  - Restful design
  - JSON-based data
  - Simple Versioning
  - Key-based access control
- The same basic APIs now support single page applications and native client user interfaces

Responding to these trends, most modern applications take an API-centric applications architecture approach following simple design tenets such as a RESTful design, JSON-based data, simply versioning, and key-based access control. And the popularity of this architectural approach grew alongside the popularity of single page applications, and also reinvigorated the native client development on mobile platforms as the same APIs can now support web and native user interfaces. Widespread adoption of these also paved way for application to application integration leveraging APIs thereby simplifying integrations.

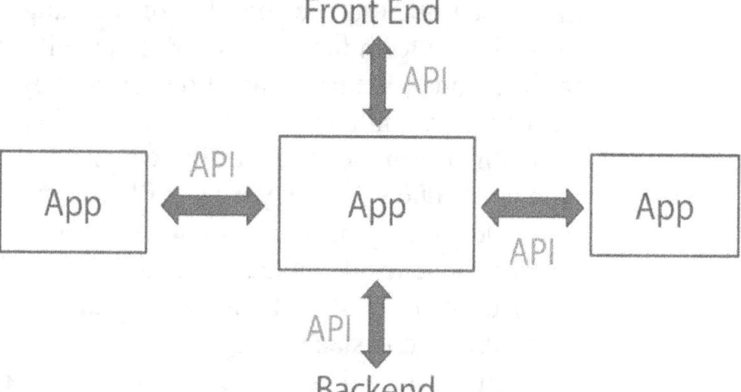

Application to application integrations leverage APIs

Some industry heavyweights such as Amazon, EBay, Google, and Netflix have gone a step further by using an architectural approach referred to as microservices architecture, which involves exploring an application into granular components of fine-grained services and using APIs as a means to glue these components together.

Microservices Architecture

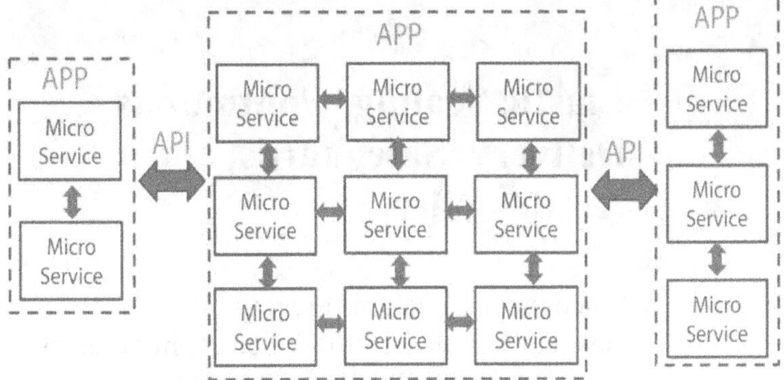

- Microservices imply composing applications with fine-grained services
- Microservices interact through well-defined APIs

These services are deployable independent of each other. Enterprises adopting such architectures also typically reorganize their teams around the microservices they develop leading to higher autonomy, greater cohesion, and quicker feedback cycle and decision-making.

Benefits of Microservices Architecture
- Development teams organized around microservices benefit from:
  - Higher autonomy
  - Greater cohesion
  - Quicker feedback cycle and decision making
- Other benefits include:
  - Fault isolation

- Auto recovery
- Lower dependencies
- Ability to scale parts of the applications selectively

Other benefits of microservices architecture include fault isolation and auto recovery, lower dependencies and hence much better responsiveness to change, ability to scale parts of the applications selectively, etc.

Elastic Scaling, Continuous Delivery, Safeguards, and Antifragility

Since the applications are deployed on elastically scalable infrastructure, in order to take advantage of these infrastructures, the applications themselves need to be architected for elastic scalability.

Shared Nothing (SN) Architecture

- Distributed computing architecture in which each node is independent and self-sufficient, and none of the nodes share memory or disk storage which could potentially cause contention

In order to avoid disc and memory contentions resulting from such scaling, applications typically follow a shared nothing architecture, which is defined as the distributed computing architecture in which each node is independent and self-sufficient, and none of the nodes share memory or disk storage which could potentially cause contention.

In-Memory Data Grids

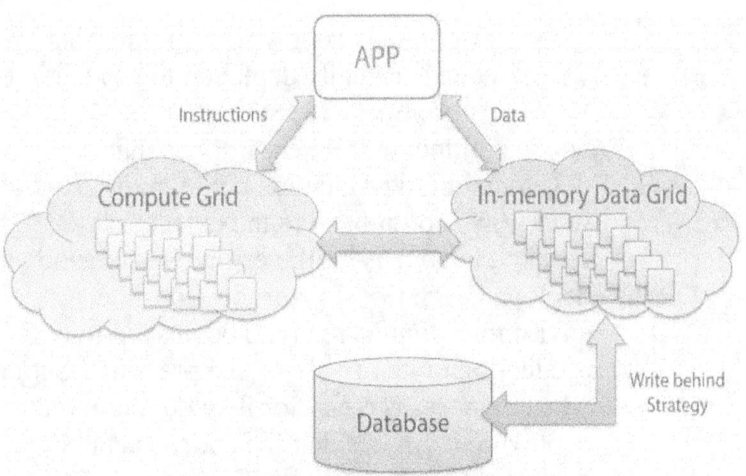

At the same time, the nodes cannot hold state. State needs to be externalized and managed through a robust and scalable in memory data grid, which can be thought of as a distributed cache on steroids. Some of the popular ones include Oracle Coherence, IBM WebSphere eXtreme Scale, GigaSpaces eXtreme Application

Platform, etc. Since the entire architecture is optimized for speed, agility, and continuous innovation, it almost goes without saying that modern business applications architecture anticipates an application development lifecycle workflow that supports either continuous delivery or continuous deployment

Continuous Delivery

- Development to production deployment workflow is optimized to the extent that the checked in code is built, verified, tested and deployed each time to a productionlike environment
- Ready to be pushed into production quite literally at the press of a button when business is ready for it

Continuous Deployment

- Continuous deployment implies that the code is actually deployed to production environment every single time

where continuous delivery implies that development to production deployment workflow is optimized to the extent that the checked in code is built, verified, tested, and deployed each time to a production-like environment and is ready to be pushed into production quite literally at the press of a button when business is ready for it, and continuous deployment implies that the code is actually deployed to production environment every single time.

Automated Deployment Pipeline

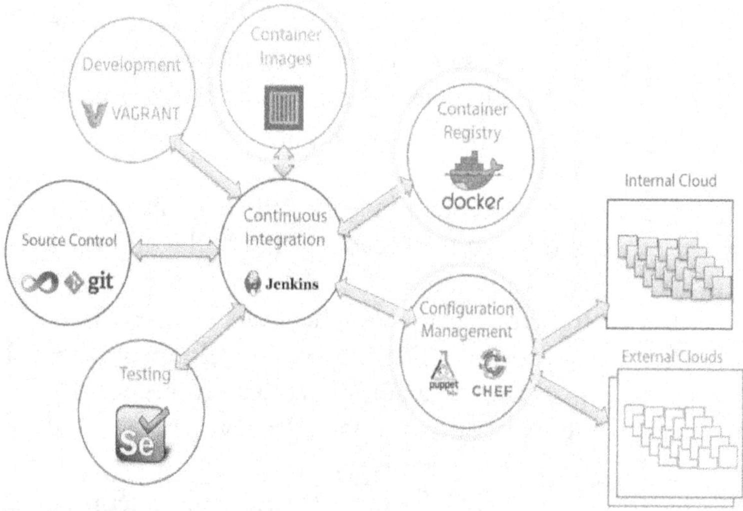

Both continuous delivery and deployment typically involves an automated deployment pipeline, which is defined as the process by which code checked into version control systems gets to the hands of the end users through various stages of testing and deployment, which in a typical enterprise brings together a number of teams in the process of scripting the sequence of steps to automate the

deployment pipeline. Containerization is a new trend in the Linux application deployment space. It is defined as a lightweight alternative to a full mission virtualization, and it involves encapsulating an application in a container with its own operating environment. This trend in container technologies, such as Docker, has lead to containers being treated as a standard unit of packaging and deployment thereby reducing the amount of complex scripting requirements to automate the process and used together with configuration management rules, such as Chef or Puppet, has the overall effect of improving the speed and quality of automated deployments. Continuous deployment, continuous innovation through experimentation, validating, and testing introduces many changes to various deployment environments, and hence there need to be certain safeguards available that enable any faults introduced inadvertently to be isolated as much as possible. This usually takes the form of continuous monitoring and health checks to ensure that the overall health of the environment is not compromised by any changes to the application or infrastructure core. Also, this requires architectural discipline to be enforced in order to prevent cascading effects of changes by actively isolating faults and also by having the capability to recover from a bad change effortlessly. Some interesting patterns that enable these architectural safeguards are discussed in Michael Nygard's book titled Release It! Design and Deploy Production-Ready Software. Antifragility is a
term coined by Nassim Taleb in a book of the same name to describe the characteristics that is the opposite of fragility. Following illustrations might describe this idea better. If you apply

stress to a system that is fragile, it breaks. If
you try to protect a system by applying robust
production measures and stop there, it creates
an illusion of stability, which will eventually be
broken by a black swan event. Some systems
get better with stress, and these kinds of
systems are referred to as antifragile.
Antifragility is a concept that is becoming
popular in the software architecture space, and
antifragility of software systems are less about
software system itself and more about the
people, process, and culture that build, support,
and enhance the systems. Antifragility in
software implies that people who build, operate,
and manage systems engage in continuous
learning and improvement of the systems
through experimentation and explorative
testing. Netflix famously uses its Simian Army
project with the famous submodule, Chaos
Monkey, which injects random failures into
production competence with the goal of
identifying and eliminating weakness in the
architecture. Agile development architecture
and DevOps culture are steps in right direction
to becoming antifragile. Adrian Cockroft, an
ex-cloud architect from Netflix who built the
highly available architecture of Netflix
platform, claimed that Netflix architecture is
built from ephemeral and often broken
competence. He describes Netflix architecture
as a service-oriented architecture based on
microservices, each of which are individually
non-essential for the operation of the whole. He
says, "When a user initiates an interaction with
the Netflix application, the action typically
invokes hundreds of connected services in the
infrastructure. If any of them fails, that piece of
functionality simply is not offered. " This
happens while the cast of the Simian Army

wreaks havoc on the infrastructure and services. Chaos Monkey disrupts on an individual server or cluster level randomly shutting down servers to make sure that automated Simians works and that redundant systems pick up the slack so constant delivery is not interrupted. Chaos Gorilla works on a larger scale by taking out entire AW zones, and Chaos Kong takes the concept to a national level by randomly shutting down the east coast or west coast regions of AWS to ensure traffic is automatically redirected to the remaining region. There are also other tools in the Simian Army. Janitor Monkey, for example, keeps everything tidy by cleaning up unused elastic compute resources. As the name implies, its job is to automatically clean up after developers. Then there is Conformity Monkey which checks for EC2 instances that are not conforming to predefined rules of best practices. Netflix lets the Simian Army roam free causing random chaos, but only Monday through Friday between the hours of 9:00 AM and 3:00 PM when managers and developers are present to address any urgent situations that might be caused inadvertently. In some cases, the tools take automated corrective actions, and in some they simply generate and alert and escalate the issue to appropriate group or individual. This kind of exploratory testing in the production environment continually proves that assailants of the environment, as well as healthy environment and architecture get better and better with every stress that it experiences, which in essence is what antifragility is all about. That brings us to the end of this module, and in summary we looked at why applications architecture is an important area of concentration for any modern enterprise. We also looked at how applications architecture fits within the larger scheme of things that concerns enterprise architecture, and we also looked at some of the trends and future directions that the industry is taking with regard to applications architecture.

Module:5 Enterprise Information Architecture

Introducing Enterprise Information Architecture

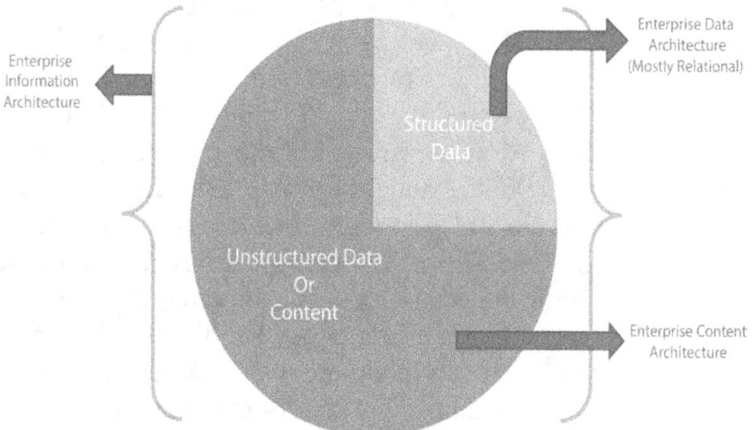

The focus of this module is enterprise information architecture, which is also referred to in some quarters as data architecture. However, for the purpose of this book, we use the phrase data architecture to refer to the discipline that deals with raw relational data while information architecture relates to a higher-level abstraction where both relational and unstructured data can be leveraged to support the information needs of the enterprise.

- Wrong decisions and misjudgements are very expensive and visible
- Organizations require effective decision support capability at all levels
- They require reports constructed from historical data
- They also need the capability to unearth hidden insights, trends, and predictive forecasts

Today's pace of business change and the overall turbulent business environment makes each wrong decisions or misjudgments at any level of the organization very expensive.

Organizations require effective decision support systems at all levels in order to gain insights through reports constructed from reliable facts and figures from past

data, insights through trend analysis and complex analytical processing, as well as predictive analysis to forecast future demands and to analyze what-if scenarios.

Information Architecture Challenges

- Information environment in most enterprises are built bottom-up without central planning or vision
- Data is scattered across multitudes of data repositories
- Data and technology capabilities are redundant across business silos, leading to high total cost of ownership
- Lack of enterprise-wide governance
- Inability to leverage and connect information across multiple systems
- Overall data quality and timeliness issues

Most enterprises encounter many serious internal challenges while attempting to build effective decision support capabilities. Some of these challenges are as follows. The information environment in most enterprises are built bottom-up to cater to local needs of a certain application or solution without a central planning or vision. Data is scattered across hundreds or even thousands of data repositories across the enterprise making it nearly impossible to keep track of them. Redundancy of data and technology across business silos contributing to high total cost of ownership. Lack of governance of information across lines of business applications, business functions, and business units leading to inability to leverage and connect information existing across systems. Data quality and timeliness issues. Compounding these existing complexities, the new business environment demand capturing data from a wide variety of sources, such as electronic sensors, RFID tags, application logs, social media emails, videos, images, and so forth. Corresponding to these wide sources of information, the volume and velocity at which the data is captured has increased tremendously as well.

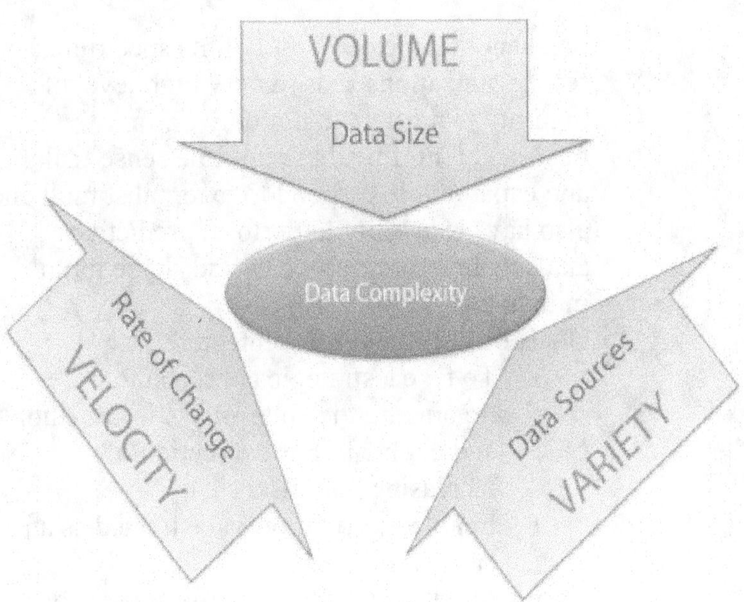

Data Complexity Is Increasing
- Businesses demand capturing data from a variety of sources such as,
  - Electronic sensors
  - RFID tags
  - Application logs
  - Social media posts, Emails
  - Videos, Images and so forth
- Not only the sources, but the volume and velocity of data has increased
- Enterprises are competing to mine insights from this data to be more agile, innovate and differentiate in marketplace

Enterprises are now competing to mine these data to gain valuable insights that would help them to respond, as well as to innovate and differentiate better in the marketplace. Across the industry, the information architecture maturity of organizations vary considerably. While a great majority of organizations still struggle to get their historical reporting accurate and reliable and within agreeable timeframes on one hand, on the other end of the spectrum, a few organizations show a very high level of maturity that caters to not only on-time historical reporting, but real-time sense-making and capability to respond to external stimuli and also have capability to perform predictive analysis in order to forecast and shape future initiatives.

Goals of Information Architecture

- To take a strategic approach to organizing the enterprise's information and evolve it in the direction of increasing maturity
- Enable information to be treated as an enterprise asset
- Making information agile and easily interoperable across
  - Applications
  - Business units
  - Organization boundaries
- Delivery high quality structured and unstructured data in formats that enable them to be integrated and analyzed in new ways

The goal of information architecture is essentially to take a strategic approach to organizing the enterprise's information and evolve it in the direction of increasing maturity in alignment with its strategic business objectives. It seeks to elevate information to be treated as an enterprise asset by identifying authoritative source of truth for all information and by making it agile and easily interoperable across applications, business units, and organization boundaries. It seeks to deliver high-quality structured and unstructured data in formats that enable them to be integrated and analyzed in interesting new ways to support and empower decision-making at all levels of the organization.

Defining Enterprise Information Architecture

Enterprise Information Architecture

- EIA is a domain of enterprise architecture that focuses on developing information-centric and technically compatible systems
- It does so by providing a consistent approach to information structure and by enabling sharing of information

So how do we define EIA? That is, enterprise information architecture. Well, EIA is a domain of enterprise architecture that focuses on developing information-centric and technically compatible systems. It does so by providing a consistent approach to information structure and by enabling sharing of information across applications, lines of businesses, and organization silos.

- Enterprise-wide principles for organizing information
- Enterprise wide information-centric
  - Architecture models
  - Standards
  - Processes
- It does so in alignment with organization's strategic business objectives and architectural vision
- Liberate information
- Remove inhibitors that prevent information sharing
- Elevate information to an enterprise class asset

It defines enterprise-wide principles for organizing information, and similarly enterprise-wide information-centric architecture models, standards, and processes that guide the evolution of the organization's information assets. It does so in alignment with organization's strategic business objectives and the overall enterprise architecture vision. The enterprise information architecture seeks to liberate information trapped in multiple of siloed application-specific information repositories, as well as by removing all inhibitors that prevent information sharing. It seeks to elevate information to be treated as an enterprise asset that can then be leveraged and used across the whole enterprise in order to promote greater business agility and responsiveness.

- Defining the technical and infrastructure capabilities and processes required to manage data and information over its lifetime
- Transform and deliver information reliably and consistently and in the form that enables enterprise-wide reuse

- Ensuring enterprise-wide compliance and regulatory requirements are met
- Enabling information governance across structured and un-structured data
- Aligning information to strategic needs of the business and thereby driving agility and responsiveness of the whole organization

It does so by defining technical and infrastructure capabilities and processes required to manage data and information over its lifetime, transforming and delivering information reliably and consistently and in the form that enables enterprise-wide reuse, ensuring enterprise-wide compliance and regulatory requirements are met, enabling information governance across structured and unstructured data, aligning information to strategic needs of business and thereby driving agility and responsiveness of the whole organization.

Profile of Enterprises With Good EIA Practices

- They enjoy greater transparency
- Greater compliance
- They have identified trusted source of truth for most information assets
- They enjoy greater accuracy and reliability of information
- They consistently define and enforce information SLAs
- Information assets are shared
- Redundancies minimized or even eliminated
- Reliable and timely information
- Data warehousing capability and real-time analytics enable superior insights

Some of the characteristics of a well-architected information-enabled enterprise are as follows. These enterprises enjoy greater transparency as the information is freed from the confines of applications and user interfaces, and as a side effect are naturally compliant to many regulations, or at least find it easier to achieve compliance. These organizations have identified trusted source of truth for most information assets that are key to the enterprise and hence are able to achieve greater accuracy and reliability of information. They are able to consistently define and monitor and enforce information-centric SLAs, that is service level agreements. Information assets are shared and redundancy of data is minimized or entirely eliminated leading to greater reuse thus optimizing on the development and ongoing maintenance and support costs. Reliable and timely information enables effective historical reporting, as well as near real-time sense-making leading to better and more responsive operational decisions. These enterprises exhibit capability to systematically capture data within the enterprise data warehouse from across multiple lines of business applications, as well as possessing the ability to process large volumes of data from a variety of sources and formats flowing at high speeds. These capabilities enable these enterprises to achieve higher levels of maturity in the information hierarchy unlocking deeper insights and affording a line of sight into future needs of the enterprise.

Data Domains

Now that we understand the motivation and drivers for enterprise information architecture and we have covered the definition of EIA, this section seeks to provide a quick overview of the key building blocks of enterprise information architecture. However, before we begin, we will need to get an understanding of the data domains within an enterprise. The core capabilities of information architecture are based on the data domains.

Data Domains

- Data domains are a classification of enterprise information based on their type and purpose
- There are five of them and are usually referred to as the five pillars of enterprise information reference model
- Information Reference Model is a domain specific ontology that defines the concepts pertaining to information architecture

Data domains are a classification of enterprise information based on their type and purpose. There are five of them and are usually referred to as the five pillars of enterprise information reference model where an information reference model is a domain-specific ontology that defines the concepts pertaining to information architecture. So then, let's get a quick overview of the data domains.

Metadata is the data about data and is the information that describes the characteristics of the enterprise data assets and other entities. It can be viewed as the collection of data and information used to measure, develop, and operate all of the enterprise information. Metadata is the foundation data domain which serves as the specification and enabler to generate instantiations of higher-level data domains. The master data domain refers to the instance of data describing core business entities. Typical master data domain entities include entities such as customer, product, account, location, contract, et cetera. These are managed within an enterprise master data management system, and since the business entities in the master data domain is highly reused across the gamut of enterprise applications, it is expected to meet high standards of accuracy, completeness, consistency, timeliness, relevance, and reliability. The specification and attribute definition of what makes up a master data entity is captured in metadata and exploited as a guideline for the master data instantiations. Operational data domain. This includes structured relational data resulting from business transactions and hence are usually fine-grained and transactional in nature. They frequently incorporate enterprise master data such as, for example, a customer order, which is a transactional data, and it incorporates master data information such as product and customer. Unstructured data domain includes all forms of data that is managed within a content-management system, as well as semi-structured data such as XML files, documents, text files, et cetera stored within enterprise repositories. Both operational and unstructured data reside at the same layer of information reference model and capture transactional information. Analytical data is usually derived by importing operational data into analytical context. Data from operational data domain is moved into dedicated analytical systems such as a data warehouse for transactional and analytical reporting. Objects of this domain could also be derived from unstructured data, master data, or metadata domains.

Building Blocks of Enterprise Information Architecture

Core Building Blocks Are Based on Data Domains

- Metadata
- Master Data
- Operational Data
- Unstructured Data
- Analytical Data

The core conceptual building blocks of enterprise information architecture are based on these data domains. That is, you would expect to have the building blocks corresponding to these data domains within an enterprise's information architecture. Let's look at each of these building blocks then.

Metadata Management – Building Block

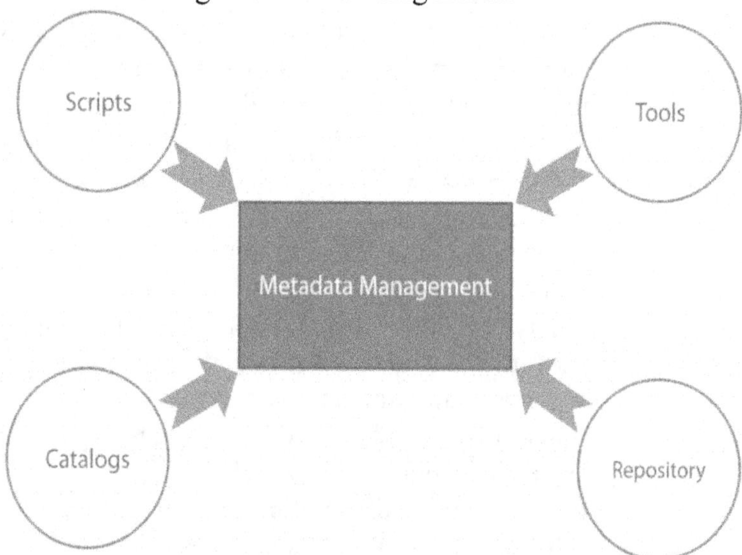

- Primarily focused on establishing an enterprise business glossary in order to correlate business and technical terms
- Forms the basis for effective information governance
- Enables the deployment of information as a strategic enterprise asset

Metadata management, which is primarily focused on establishing an enterprise's business glossary in order to correlate business and technical terms. It forms the basis for effective information governance and enables the deployment of information as a strategic enterprise asset.

Master Data Management – Building Block

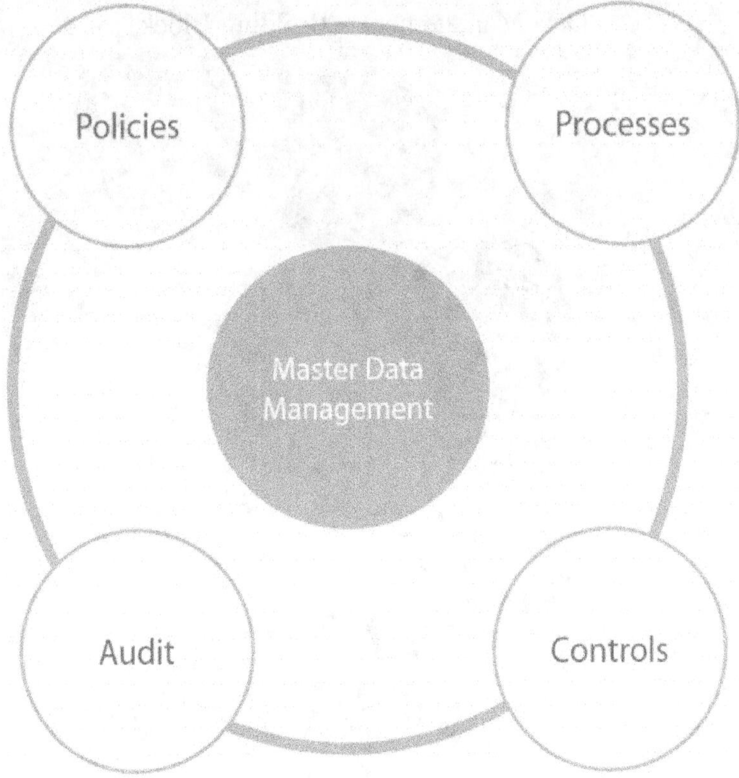

- Creates an authoritative source of Master Data
- Lays the foundation to establish guidelines for lifecycle management of Master Data
- Enables centralized quality control, and enforcement of business rules, access privileges

Master data management. This building block creates an authoritative source of master data within an enterprise using an MDM solution, that is a master data management solution, thus laying the foundation to establish guidelines for effective management of master data. It is an important piece that enables centralized quality control and enforcement of business rules, access privileges, et cetera.

Data Management – Building Block

- The data management capability provides all functions needed by transactional systems to manage structured operational data across its lifecycle

Data management. The data management capability provides all functions needed by transactional systems, such as order entry or billing applications, to manage structured operational data across its lifecycle.

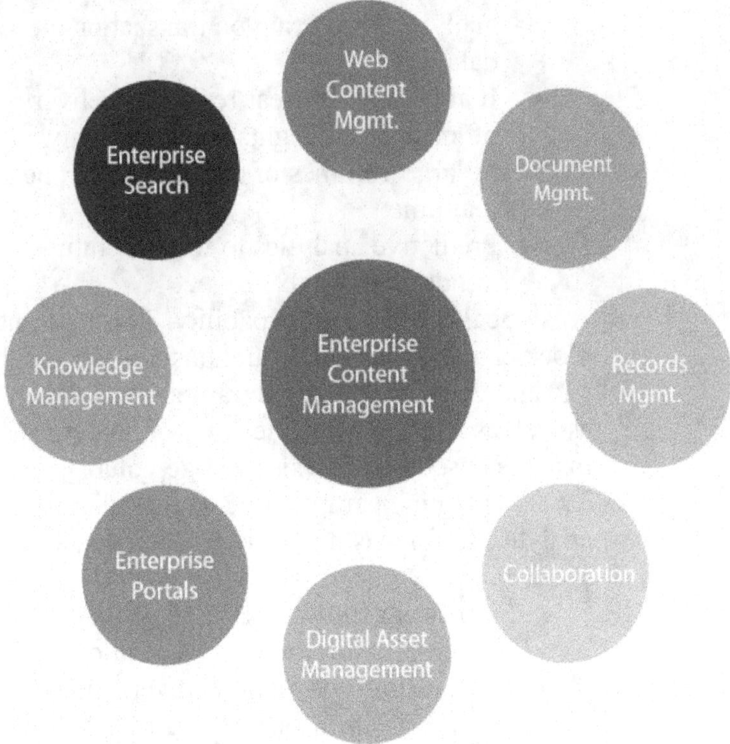

This building block enables end-to-end management of unstructured data

Enterprise content management. This building block enables end-to-end management of unstructured data. This is particularly important in industries which has high level of compliance and records management requirements.

Analytical Applications – Building Block
- Analytical Capabilities Building Block
  - Data Exploration
  - Online analytical processing
  - Geospatial data processing
  - Agile Analytics
  - Big data integration
  - Application development

- This building block enables both datawarehousing, historical and analytical reporting on transactional data
- It also supports near real-time delivery of analytical insights based on analysis of large volumes of data flowing in near real time
- Predictive analytics to forecast future trends, events etc.

Analytical applications capability. This building block enables both data warehousing, historical and analytical reporting on transactional data, as well as near real-time delivery of analytical insights based on analysis of large volumes of data flowing in near real time, and predictive analytics to forecast future trends, events, and so forth.

Other Significant Building Blocks of EIA
- Enterprise Information Integration
- Enterprise Information Governance
- Enterprise Information Security & Privacy

In addition to these core capabilities, enterprises also typically incorporate the following three building blocks: enterprise information integration, enterprise information governance, and enterprise information security and privacy.

Enterprise Information Integration - Block
- Extraction, Transformation & Load (ETL)
- Enterprise Application Integration (EAI)
- Enterprise Service Bus (ESB)

Enterprise information integration. This building block is realized through the following sub-building blocks: extraction, transformation, and load capability, enterprise application integration capability, and enterprise service bus capability. It enables the enterprise to

understand, cleanse, transform, and deliver data throughout its lifecycle. It enables data harmonization from various operational data sources into an enterprise-wide data warehouse.
Information Governance – Building Block

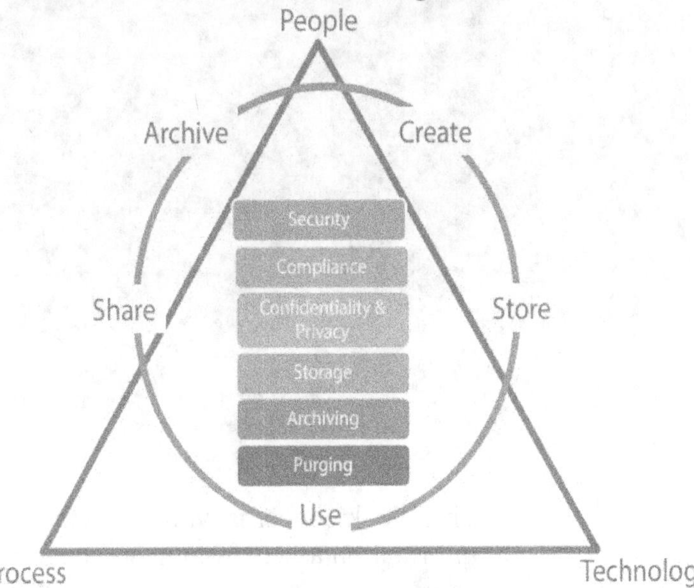

Information governance enables a business to manage and govern its information as strategic assets, and it is important for the design, deployment, and control processes of an instantiation of enterprise information architecture throughout its lifecycle.
Information Security and Privacy - Block

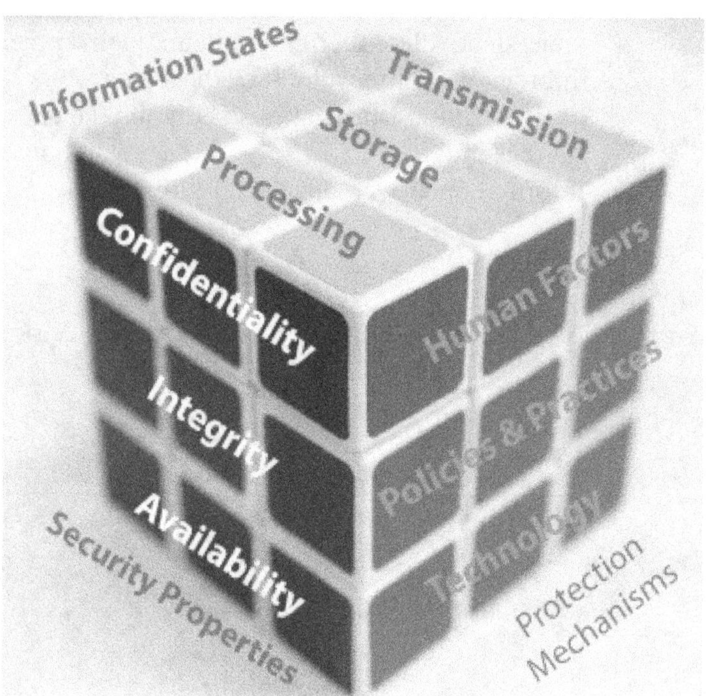

- This block concerns with protecting information assets from unauthorized access
- Minimizing the probability of loss of mission critical information
- Information privacy among other things enable a company to comply legal regulations

Information security and privacy where information security concerns with protecting information assets from unauthorized access, which prevents the probability of loss of mission-critical information. Information privacy enables a company to comply, for example, with legal regulations protecting the privacy of personally identifiable information.

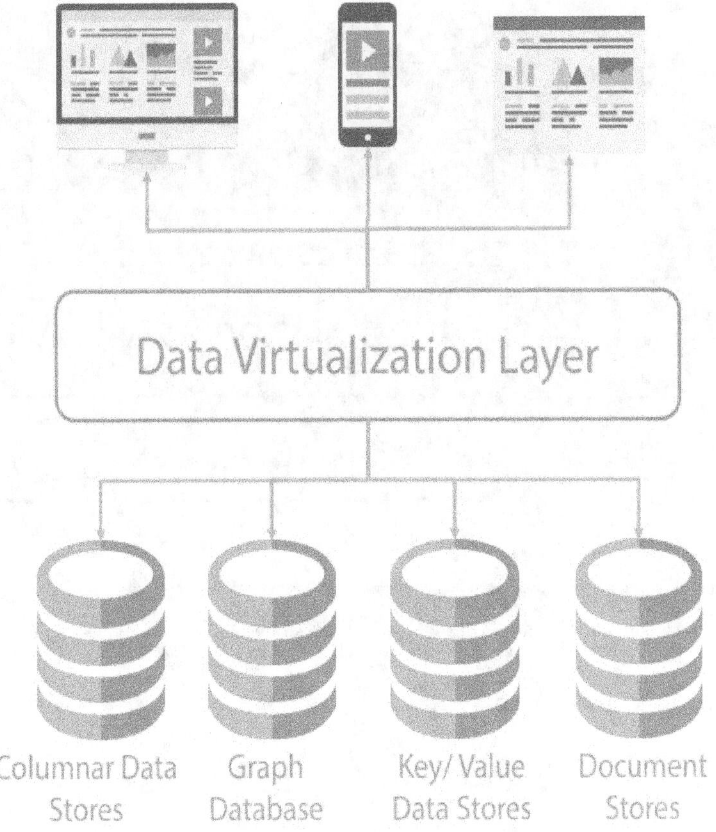

- Data virtualization enables applications to retrieve and manipulate data without requiring details such as its formatting or location

Some of the more proactive enterprises with more advanced vision and roadmap for enterprise information architecture also have more modern building blocks incorporated, such as data virtualization capability, which enables applications to retrieve and manipulate data without requiring details about the data such as how it is formatted or where it is physically located.

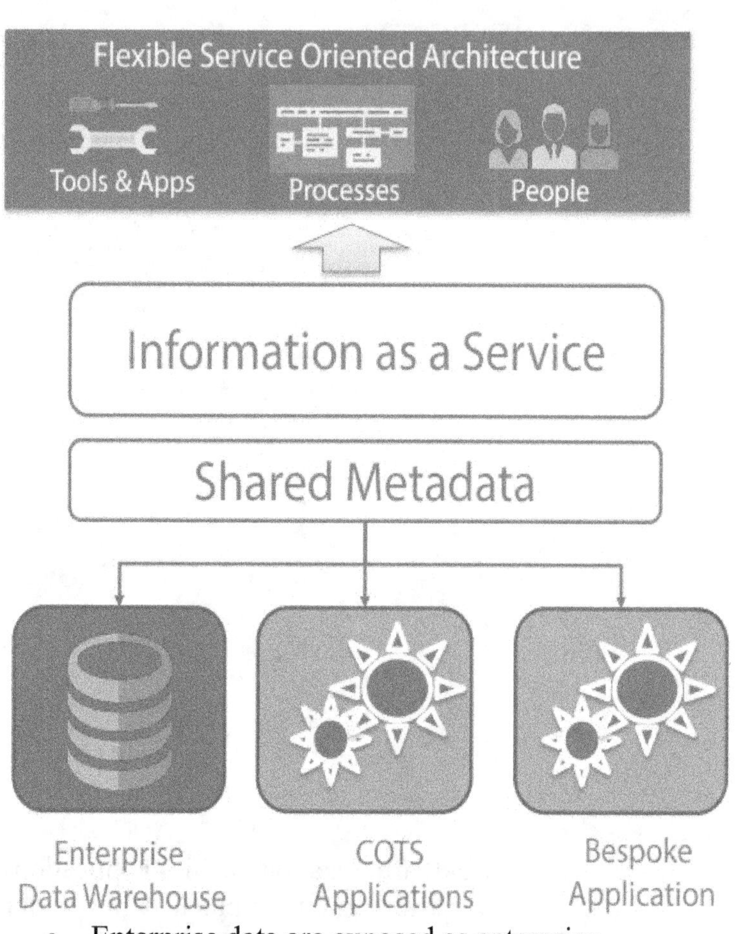

- Enterprise data are exposed as enterprise services Made available for virtually any application

Information as a Service. With Information as a Service, sources of enterprise data are exposed as enterprise services and made available for consumption by virtually any application that needs them.

Data Mashup – Building Block

- Mashups typically use web 2.0 architecture
- REST based APIs and lightweight integration techniques such as JSON, RSS, AJAX etc.
- Key Drivers Include:
    - Empowering end-users to create the insights they need
    - Reduce the dependence on IT and enabling business users to work with data directly

Data mashup capability. Through this capability, enterprises effectively allow end users to access information from multiple independent sources through a web application to creatively uncover and produce new innovative insights. Mashups typically use web

2. 0 architecture using REST=based APIs and lightweight integration techniques, such as JSON, RSS, or AJAX. The key drivers for adoption and use of these technologies are, number one, to empower end users to create the insights they need by merging together data from both internal and external sources, to reduce dependance on IT and enabling business users to work with data directly through a self-service channel and produce insights they need cost-effectively.

Other EIA Building Blocks

- Cloud Computing
- Big Data

Cloud computing and big data are other capabilities that information architecture seeks to leverage. However, they are discussed in more details subsequently in module seven. With that, we conclude this quick overview of enterprise information architecture.

Quick Recap

- We began by looking at forces and business drivers for enterprise information architecture and the high level goals
- A working definition of enterprise information architecture and some of the characteristics of a well architected information enabled enterprise
- Then we looked at the enterprise data classification that defines the five key data domains
- Finally we covered the key building blocks of enterprise information architecture that you find in an enterprise

To recap, in this module we began by looking at forces and business drivers for enterprise information architecture and the high-level goals. We then looked at a working definition of enterprise information architecture and some of the characteristics of a well-architected information-enabled enterprise. Then we looked at the enterprise's data classifications that defines the five key data domains. Finally, we covered the key building blocks of enterprise information architecture that you would find in a typical enterprise.

Module:6 Infrastructure Architecture

Introduction

The current module will provide a quick overview of infrastructure architecture, which is also referred to as technology architecture by some.

Module Focus

- Data Centers
- Servers
- Networking
- Storage
- End User Devices
- Industry Trends

We will go through the following major building blocks: data center, servers, network, storage, end user devices, and followed by a section to discuss some of the key trends in the IT infrastructure architecture space.

Data Centers

So let's take a quick lap around each of the building blocks beginning with the data center. Evolving from the large mainframe- based computer rooms of previous decades, today's data centers have grown in sophistication and in many instances in size to meet the much expanded and continually evolving information needs of modern enterprise and its customers.
Key Data Centre Building Blocks
- Racks
- Cabling & Patching
- Power Supply
- Environment Control Systems
- Fire Suppression
- Layout and Physical Structure

Following constitute the significant building blocks of the data centers: the racks, cabling and patching, power supply, environment control systems, fire suppression systems, and the layout and physical structure of the data center itself.
Racks
- Standardized enclosures that house IT infrastructure - usually 19 inches wide
- Rack-mountable equipment are designed specifically to be placed on the racks
    - Front panel is 19 inches or 49 cm wide
    - Their height is measure in multiples of "Rack Units" denoted by letter 'U' (1.752 inches or 44.5 mm)
    - Industry standard rack is 42 U high

The racks are standardized and usually 19 inches wide enclosures that house IT infrastructure components. The equipments designed to be placed on the racks matches this width, and their heights are measured in rack units denoted by the letter U where a U is 1. 752 inches or 44. 5 mm. An industry standard rack cabinet is 42 Us in height. Cabling. Lack of discipline in cabling can cause the data center to descend into chaos and confusion very quickly.

Standard Cabling -TIA 942

- The Telecom Industry Association's Telecommunications Infrastructure Standard (TIA 942)
- Adhering to standards enables
    - Standard and consistent nomenclature
    - Failsafe operation
    - Reliability
    - Expandability & Scalability
    - Robust protections

Telecommunications Infrastructure Standard, referred to as TIA 942, represent the best practices in data center cabling and provides the advantage of consistent nomenclature, fail-safe operation, long-term reliability, expandability, scalability, and protection against overheating and fire-related risks.

Power Supply

- Foundational infrastructure capability supported by a Data Centre
- Represents one of the highest operating expense
- Power density and quality of power supplied are important considerations
- Data centers use a combination of:
    - Redundant utility power sources,

- Uninterrupted Power Supply (UPS) and
- Backing power generators

Power supply is a foundational infrastructure capability supported by a data center and represents one of the highest operating expense of running the data center. Power density requirements and the quality of power supply are the key considerations here. A combination of redundant utility power sources, UPS, and backing power generators are used to provide power supply to data centers. The recurring cost of powering large data centers represent a significant motivation for enterprises to look for greener strategic alternatives.

Environment Control System

- Heat - 90% of all power used by the IT equipment are converted into heat
- Humidity and dust control are other problems
- Data centers use a combination of :
  - Precision cooling,
  - Air quality control systems,
  - Limited manual access policies

Environment Control Systems. About 90% of all power used by IT equipment are converted into heat which need to be dissipated by a cooling system to avoid overheating, and this represents the top environment control problem for the data center, followed by humidity and dust control. A combination of precision cooling and air quality control systems and measures to limit or award physical human access to systems are used in data centers to maintain an ideal condition.

Fire Suppression

- Fire prevention involves
  - Prevention of equipment and cable overheating

- Use of physical firewall
- Use of fire resistant materials
- Fire detection involves
  - Deploying heat and fire detection systems
- Fire suppression involves
  - Reducing oxygen levels
  - Deploying water sprinklers

Fire suppression is an important measure that needs to be undertaken in the data centers, and it involves prevention of equipment and cable overheating; use of physical firewalls around the data centers, as well as using fire resistant materials for the floors, ceilings, and walls of the data center; deploying heat and fire detection systems which can detect fire early enough to provide opportunity for suppressing it; and finally using active suppression methods when a major fire incident does occur, such as reducing the oxygen from the air by using an inert gas mixture such as argon and nitrogen and deploying water sprinklers to avoid damages and loss of life. These constitute the key methods by which fire suppression is implemented in data centers.

Layout & Structure

- Equipment density is a key consideration
- Preventing intrusion and fire are important too
- So is serviceability and enabling human access

The layout of the data center, its floors, walls, windows, doors, ducting, and pipeline for gas and water all require planning and architectural consideration. Current and future equipment density requirement is a key influence on decisions around layout, cabling, and cooling systems. Preventing intrusion and fire are important considerations as well, and so is the serviceability and provisioning of human access to systems. That brings us to the end of a very quick overview of the data center building block.

Servers

Server Building Blocks
- CPU
- Memory
- Buses & Interfaces
- Network connectivity
- Internal Power Supply

Servers constitute the compute engines of the enterprise IT infrastructure, and they execute a wide range of applications for the enterprise. The CPU, memory, buses and interfaces, network interface cards, and the internal power supply form the major components of a server. CPUs are characterized by its microarchitecture, that is its physical design, its instruction set architecture, which is teleological architecture which abstracts a physical CPU architecture from the layers above; the word size, which defines the amount of data that can be read or returned by the processor at any one time; and the clock speed, which indicates the number of process of cycles that can be back in a single second. The memory in the context of a server can be considered a hierarchy of information storage capability implemented using multiple technologies ranging from CPU registers integrated into the processors, caches, random access memory, local hard disk to network attached storage, storage area networks, and even cloud-based storages. Buses are a set of wires that serve as an electronic signaling pathway that interconnects the server components. There are two kinds of buses, internal bus, which are also referred to as system bus, and external or expansion bus. System bus connects components on the motherboard, such as the CPU and main memory, and the external bus connects the CPU to external devices that expands the capability of the server. Expansion bus are exposed via interfaces. Interfaces can be both internal and external. Internal interfaces such as ISA, MCI, PCI, or PCIE connect components to server motherboard. The external interfaces such as USB and Thunderbolt connect external devices. Network interface cards are an example of expansion cards, and they can connect to the motherboard via the ISA, PCI, or PCIE interfaces, or be integrated directly into the server motherboard chipset. The role of the internal power supply unit is to convert the utility delivered power to data current voltage as required by various components within the server. In order to avoid a single point of failure, it is important to have redundant power supply units for servers, hence even entry level servers typically support dual power supplies. Before we wind up the discussion on the server block, let's do a quick roundup of the server marketplace. The server marketplace can be broadly classified into four groups of servers. X86 processor-based servers are at present the most dominant server processors in the industry. As of mid 2014, about 95% of all installed servers use a variation of the x86 architecture. According to Gartner, 92% of all servers shipped in 2013 were Intel x86 processors. The largest vendors of x86 processors are Intel and AMD, and the largest vendor of the x86 servers are HP, Dell, and Lenovo. Mainframes are high performance servers made for high volume processor-intensive computing. IBM, Unisys, Bull, Fujitsu, and NEC are the major vendors in this space. Contrary to the common views, mainframes are an evolving platform, and the modern mainframes are a viable option to power the enterprise's compute needs. Mid-range servers are positioned between the mainframe and typical x86 servers. Oracle SPARC-based systems and IBM Power series processor-based systems are good examples of servers in this category. SoC, or system on a chip architectures such as ARM and Intel Atom series of processors are considered attractive options for low-end server space. It is a budding platform as of today, but it could grow fast propelled by its promise of low power footprint. That completes the market roundup, as well as this quick overview of the server building block.

Networking

Computer networks are a vital part of any enterprise's IT infrastructure. Let's take a quick look at some of the constituents of this building block that makes it work. Broadly speaking, computer networks can be classified as LAN and WAN where LAN is a local area network built privately by an organization while WAN, or wide area network, spans large distances and hence require the use of a telecom service provider infrastructure to connect. International

Standards Organization's OSI, that is Open System Interconnect model, is usually used to comprehend the technology components of a network, although in real world you would rarely find networks implementing all the protocol layers of the OSI model. The basic idea behind the model is that the end-to-end communication infrastructure between the sending and receiving applications are split into seven layers along the lines of key responsibilities. Each layer functions like a black box to layers above it and facilitates certain aspect of the network communication. The metadata added by a layer is attached to chunks of information at the transmission end which will be used by the network infrastructure to route it to its destination. This requests the corresponding layers at two ends of the communication to use the same networking protocol, which is kind of conveyed by the color codes used here. The physical media, or the physical link, is the actual media used to transport the network communication signals. Many kinds of physical media are in use today including twisted-pair cables, fiber optic cables, co-axial cables, radio waves, micro waves, as well as satellite-based communication. Physical layer. The physical layer defines electrical and physical specification for
devices including physical interfaces to various media, voltage specifications, network topologies, et cetera. Modems, network interface cards, and network hubs are examples of some of the devices that enable this layer. Data link layer provides the protocols that would enable data to be transferred between network nodes local to the network. It does so using an addressing method tied to the hardware called the MAC addresses. Network

switches are an example of devices that enable this layer. Network layer defines how interconnected networks works out the routes taken by data packet from source destination between connected networks. Network routers are an important component that enable this layer. Transport layer provides abstraction to lower level layers, as well as allows multiplexing, that is converting data from multiple applications into a single network stream, and demultiplexing, which is the opposite process of multiplexing, across multiple applications and ensures reliability where required. Session layer enables establishment of persistent logical links across networks at an application level enabling exchange of data between applications. Presentation layer enables presenting data to application layer in the desired format. Audio, video, file codecs, encoding formats of files are examples of protocol that enable the presentation layer. Application layer is the top-most layer of the OSI model exposing application layer protocols directly used by the application, such as HTTP, SMTP, et cetera. That brings us to the end of the overview of the networking building block.

Storage

Storage Building Blocks
- Storage Media
- Storage Interface Protocols
- Storage Networks
- Storage Optimization Technologies

In this section, we will quickly explore the storage building block which is a key enterprise

infrastructure component. We will explore this building block along the lines of the storage media, the storage interface protocols, storage networks, and storage optimization technologies. Storage media refers to the actual medium used for the storage of data. Broadly, the media can be categorized as random access and sequential access storage devices. Examples of random access storages include magnetic storage disks such as hard disks, and optical storage media such as CDs, DVDs, and Blu-ray disks, as well as flash memory-based solid-state devices. The hard disks are the primary workhorse of the enterprise storage infrastructure. Strictly speaking, the term hard disk refers to the electromechanical devices that have rotating platters of rigid disks on which data is read and written magnetically using a movable read/write head. However, this term is now being used to refer to flash memory- based solid-state devices as well, which are manufactured in the same form factor and supports the same interface protocols as an electromechanical hard disk device. While the best example of sequential media are the various forms of magnetic tape-based storage devices because data can only be read and written in one direction, and since it allows only sequential access of data, this kind of media is typically used for long- term archiving of enterprise data, that is for retention periods ranging from 10 to 30 years.
Storage Interface Protocols

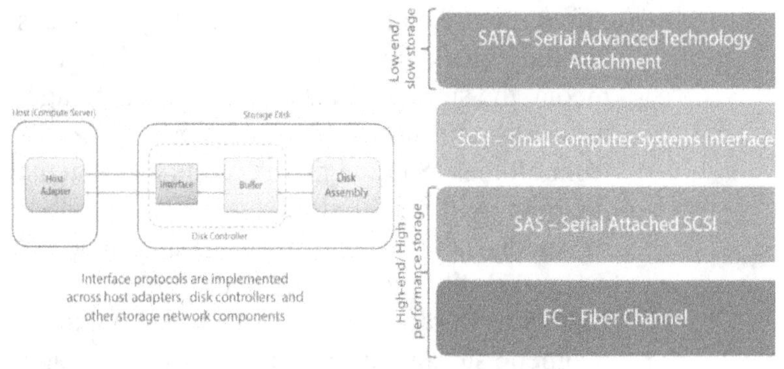

The storage media need to communicate and work in sync with the compute server, and this is enabled through interface protocols, which, depending on the protocol, are implemented across servers, disk controllers, and other storage infrastructure. The popular ones applicable to servers are SATA, or Serial Advanced Technology Attachment, SCSI, or Small Computer System Interface, SAS, or Serial Attached SCSI, and FC, which stands for Fiber Channel. In general, today the enterprise market is predominantly split between SAS, Fiber Channel, and SATA, SATA being used for low-end cost capacity optimized storages while high performance storages are delivered using SAS and FC interfaces. Storage networks. From an enterprise infrastructure perspective, storages attached directly to servers are not easily shared across the infrastructure, and it's also difficult to manage and optimize. This led to the evolution of two storage network technologies, which are storage area networks, or SAN, and network attached storages referred to as NAS. SANs are high speed dedicated network of storage arrays where a storage array is a server that hosts shared storage devices. This enables compute servers to access storage blocks over a network, thereby supporting consolidation of storage and facilitating centralized data management. SANs meet the enterprise storage demands efficiently with better economies of scale and also provides effective maintenance and protection of data. SAN vs. NAS

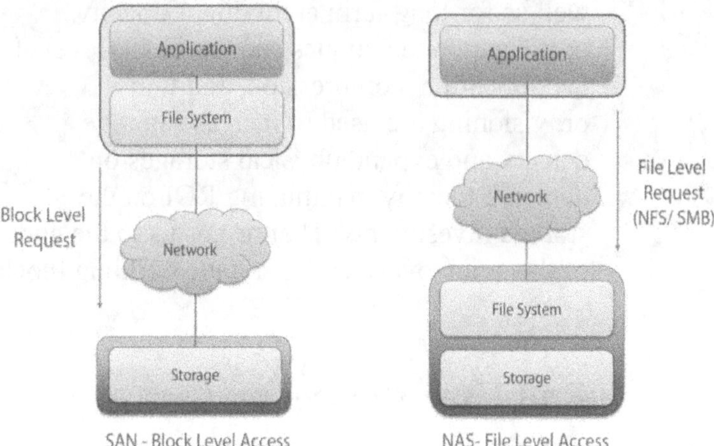

While SAN abstracts storage access at the level of raw storage I/O blocks, NAS are typically implemented as appliances that exposes file system to the servers over the network. NAS is typically used for storing unstructured data and uses NFS and SMB protocols to serve Linux and Windows environments respectively.
Optimization Techniques

- Availability and resilience improved using RAID techniques
- Replication supports disaster recovery and business continuity
- Snapshot and cloning used for efficient backups
- Block-level deduplication, compression and thin-provisioning maximize storage density

Many techniques are used to improve storage efficiency, availability, resilience to failure, and data security. The availability and resilience of storage systems are improved using RAID techniques. Further techniques such as data replication are employed with a view to support disaster recovery and business continuity, and techniques such as snapshot and cloning are employed for efficient and seamless backups, as well as for long-term archiving. Capacity optimization techniques such as block-level deduplication, compression, and thin provisioning are used to increase storage density and expand physical storages on demand, thereby maximizing ROI on the storage investments. That brings us to the end of the quick overview of storage building block.

End User Devices

End User Devices
  * Workstations (Desktops and Laptops)
  * Tablets and Mobile Devices
  * Virtualization (Desktop and Application)

Let's explore the end-user devices building block of the enterprise infrastructure. Although this block technically covers all devices used by the enterprise workforce, this overview applies more to the following items: workstations, which are comprised of desktops and laptops, tablets and mobile devices, desktop and application virtualization.

Workstations
  * Primary end-user workstation within enterprise is predominantly an x86 based workstation
  * About 90% of them run on a version of Microsoft Windows as of March 2015
  * Typically laptops are considered a higher risk category than desktops

- Laptops are more vulnerable to
  - cyber attacks
  - physical damages
  - being lost or stolen

The primary end-user workstation within the enterprise is still predominantly an x86 based workstation, which typically is either a desktop or a corporate laptop with upwards of 90% of them running on a version of Microsoft Windows as of March 2015. While desktop workstations are usually secure and confined within office space and are usually inside a corporate network, laptops are higher risk items with greater vulnerability to cyber attacks, physical damages, and are more likely to be lost or stolen owing to the fact that it is moved around quite a bit.

Bring Your Own Devices (BYOD)

- Influx of employee owned personal mobile devices in their environment further adds to the complexity
- Many devices are not actively managed by the enterprise
- Positives:
  - Productive and motivated employees
- Negatives:
  - Exposure to security risks increases dramatically

This challenge is further accentuated with enterprises having to deal with an influx of employee owned personal mobile devices in their environment. Contrary to the preference of enterprise IT in the context of bring your own device scenario, many of these devices remain unmanaged, although the employees use it to access corporate applications, emails, and documents. The positive side of this trend is that employees tend to be happier, motivated, and much more productive working on devices of their choice and using tools and apps of their choice which keeps the work moving forward independent of the location they are at. However, the negative side of this is that the enterprise IT feels more exposed and vulnerable to security risks caused by these trends. These trends imply that the challenges of an effective end-user computing is driven by an urgent need for IT to get a firm handle on managing and securing all devices used for accessing and working on enterprise data and information thereby effectively managing risks, enforcing compliance, and

managing costs and complexity. And secondly, to achieve this without intruding into employee's freedom of device choice and flexibility, providing a secure and consistent access to applications and providing consistent experience across devices to keep them productive and motivated. Many organizations have responded to this trend by embracing the new vision to enable employees to remain productive working from anywhere on any device while many others have taken cautious first steps to include mobility alongside a predominantly workstation and laptop-centric environment.

User / Devices Management and Configuration Products

- Environments based on pre-configured images
- Register personal devices with IT
- Access corporate resource on premise and over internet
- Setup access policies
- Continuous access to devices for servicing and management
- Granular control of access

- Encryption of data
- Selective wiping of corporate data
- Airwatch (a VMware company), Citrix, IBM, Good Technology and Microsoft

Correspondingly, a range of enterprise technologies are available on the menu to architect an effective end-user computing environment which include device management and configuration products and tools which help create end user environments based on preconfigured images, capability to enable end-users to register their personal devices with IT, and enable them to connect and access corporate resources through those devices both on premise and over the internet. These tools enable setting up of effective access policies based on their business requirements that not only considers who the user is, but also which device he's working on, corporate resource he is trying to access, and which network he's accessing the corporate resources from. And also support more advanced capabilities such as enabling continuous access to devices for servicing and management, granular control of access to apps and data, encryption of data in the network and on devices, selective wiping of corporate data from devices, et cetera. Some of the leading vendors in this space include Airwatch, which is a VMWare company, Citrix, IBM, Good Technology, and Microsoft.

Application delivery technologies/ tools

- Apps installed from public app stores
- Enterprise-specific app stores hosted privately
- Zero footprint virtualized applications
- Virtual desktop infrastructure
- Desktop as a Service
- Cloud-hosted or on premise web-based applications

Application delivery tools and technologies are also a significant component of end-user computing building block, and they enable a range of application delivery options including native apps to be installed from public app stores or accessing and self-installing apps from enterprise-specific app stores hosted privately, virtualized applications executed on the server and streamed to end-user devices requiring zero footprint on the device, client and server-based virtual desktop infrastructure, virtual desktop services from Desktop as a Service providers, or plain old web-based applications accessed via browsers.

Identity & Access Management

- Single user identity across enterprise resources on premise and in cloud
    - Federation, single and same sign-on
    - Multi-factor user authentication and device authentication
- Granular and dynamic authorizations
- Microsoft, Oracle, IBM, Octa and Ping Identity are dominant vendors

Other components of this building block include identity and access management solutions and strategies which aim to create a single user identity across enterprise resources located on premise or in the cloud through federation and support of technologies such as single sign-on and same sign-on, as well as supporting multifactor user authentication and device authentication as required for elevated security needs. With the proliferation of enterprise mobility, these tools also support granular and dynamic authorization technologies based on multiple context of the usage such as the user's role, device that he is accessing from, resources required, network accessed from, et cetera. Dominant vendors in this space include Microsoft, Oracle, IBM, as well as Octa and Ping Identity. That concludes the quick roundup of the end-user devices building block.

Industry Trends

Demands on Modern IT Infrastructure Teams Are Multifold
- Achieve more within ever shrinking time-frame and budgets
- Enterprises need flexible and agile IT infrastructure
- Uptake of web-scale IT in a big way is predicted in the near future

The demands and pressure on enterprise IT infrastructure teams are multifold. The IT infrastructure teams are required to achieve more within ever- shrinking timeframes and budgets, and this requires a flexible and agile IT infrastructure. The indications and predictions from leading industry analysts such as Gartner is that enterprises will take up web-scale IT in a big way in near future. This section will explore this trend in some detail.

What Is Web-scale IT?
- Architectural response to modern business demands on IT infrastructure
- Recognizes that traditional lead-times of weeks and months are not viable anymore
- Emulates the architectural approaches used by large cloud and web-based enterprises

- Intent is to dramatically increase the speed and agility within enterprise IT infrastructure space
- Gartner predicts that by 2017 about 50% of worlds enterprises will embrace web-scale IT

What is web-scale IT? Web-scale IT is the IT infrastructure architecture's response to an increasingly dynamic and fast-changing nature of today's business that demands greater agility. It takes cognizance of the fact that traditional enterprise release cycles and the lead times of weeks and months required to make changes to IT infrastructure may no longer be viable to keep pace with the business agility needs of the organization. It involves emulating the architectural approaches, processes, and practices used by large cloud and web- based enterprises such as Amazon, Google, Facebook, Netflix, et cetera within the enterprise IT infrastructure. The intent is to dramatically increase the speed and agility with which IT infrastructure and services can be created, configured, and made available to the business for hosting and scaling business applications. Gartner predicts that by 2017 about 50% of the world's enterprise will embrace web-scale IT. Combination of Technologies and Products

- Virtualization
- Convergence, Hyper-convergence & SDDC
- Hybrid Cloud

A combination of technologies, methods, tools, and techniques need to come together, as well as build on top of each other to make web-scale IT possible. Some of these technologies include virtualization, convergence, hyper-convergence and SDDC, stands for software-defined data centers, and hybrid cloud. Let's start exploring each of these beginning with virtualization. Virtualization of an IT resource can generally be defined as a layer of software abstraction built over the physical resource that facilitates a level of indirection that then affords greater flexibility in how the resource is utilized. Web-scale IT involves virtualizing servers, storage arrays, and networking components. Let's look at each of these.

Server Virtualization

Server Virtualization

Server virtualization has been known in the mainframe world since the '60s; however, it really caught on to the x86 platforms in the early 2000s. Server virtualization is fundamentally about introducing a software abstraction layer between the operating system and the physical server which allows a single physical server to host multiple virtual machines. Each of them can then independently run on an operating system of their own. The virtualization layer isolates virtual machines from each other and also abstracts the physical host.

Server Virtualization - Advantages

- Consolidate underutilized physical servers

- Flexibility in creating, configuring and repurposing servers
- Move virtual machines between physical servers without downtime
- Load balancing, lock-stepping, conserving power based on actual usage
- Simplified management – enabling single admin managing >1000 virtual machines
- VMware, Citrix and Microsoft are major vendors

This enables consolidating many underutilized physical servers and also affords tremendous flexibility offered by virtualization when it comes to creating, configuring, changing, and repurposing servers. Ability to represent virtual machine instances as physical files affords the flexibility to move the virtual machines between physical servers without having a downtime and therefore lending itself to many creative runtime optimization strategies such as for load balancing, lock-stepping, conserving power utilization based on actual usage pattern, et cetera. The management of server instances is much simplified enabling a single administrator to manage between 1000 and 2000 virtual machines. Major vendors in the server virtualization space include VMWare, Citrix, and Microsoft. Data storage has always been virtualized at multiple levels. File system itself is in fact a

virtualization of storage blocks, and so are rate technologies, for example, and these have been in existence for a very long time.

Storage Virtualization

- Storage virtualization is the virtualization of the storage arrays using a storage controller

- Storage controller can be a virtualization appliance or software
- Storage controller aggregates the physical storage arrays in a pool and creates a logical storage

However, the storage virtualization we are talking about here is the virtualization of the storage arrays using a storage controller which can be a virtualization appliance or a software. The storage controller aggregates the physical storage arrays in a pool and creates a logical storage which then is allocated to the compute servers as required.

Storage Virtualization - Advantages

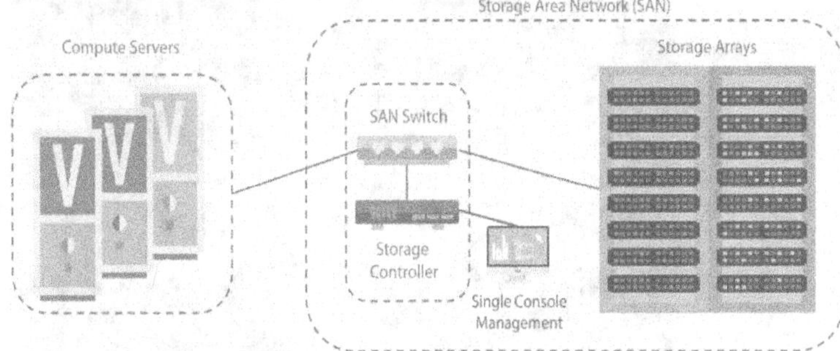

- Single console management of diverse technologies
- Greatly improved capacity utilization
- High-speed in-band caches
- Flexible data migration, dynamic tiered storage
- And other strategies for holistic optimization
- DataCore, EMC, IBM, FalconStore and NetApp are some vendors

Some of the benefits storage virtualization brings to the table include easy, single console management of storage arrays based on diverse technologies and offerings by different vendors, dramatic increase in the capacity utilization by employing techniques such as thin

provisioning, increased performance by introducing high speed caches over slower discs, improved flexibility in migrating data, implementing dynamic and tiered storage strategies for dynamic and
holistic optimization of enterprise's storage while maintaining complete transparency to compute servers. DataCore, EMC, IBM, FalconStor, and NetApp are some of the vendors in this category.

Network Functions Virtualization (NFV)

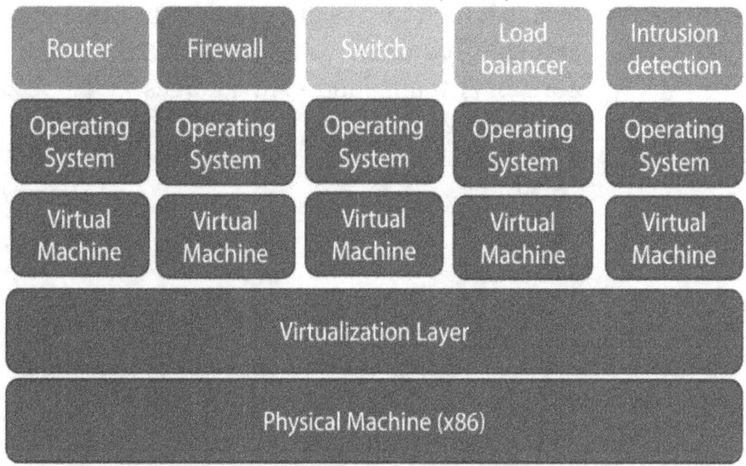

Networking functions virtualization, or NFV, involves applying the principles of server virtualization to network devices, or in other words replacing dedicated network devices and appliances such as routers, firewalls, switches, load balancers, intrusion detection, and prevention systems with virtual instances of these running inside virtual machines.

NFV - Advantages

- Large scale consolidation of physical network devices and appliances
- Reduced investment in network infrastructure
- Reduced ongoing operating costs
- Biggest benefits though are:

- network infrastructure agility and
- flexibility to repurpose and reuse investments

The benefits include large scale consolidation of physical network devices and appliances into fewer general purpose physical servers using standard server virtualization tools. The direct consequence of this is massive reduction in the investment if you are planning to acquire new network devices. Besides that, it also lowers the ongoing operational expenses of the data center by reducing the amount of rack space, power, and cooling needs. The even great benefit is achieved through flexibility, agility, and manageability that this technology offers making it possible to create, configure, delete and
reconfigure virtual networking components on demand to cater to emerging needs of the enterprise. That leads our discussion to convergence, or more specifically, converged IT infrastructures.

Convergence

Traditional IT Infrastructure Is Organized Into Silos

- Changes requires coordination, planning and are error prone
- Leads to delays in the order of weeks and months
- These impact business agility
- Enterprises are keen to converge infrastructure to support greater agility

Traditional IT infrastructure tend to be managed by teams that specialize on individual domains, that is compute, networks, storage, etc. Changes to these infrastructure based on requirements by various enterprise projects often require redesigning, planning, and coordination across these traditional silos and are error prone often leading to delays in the order of several months. These factors can be a stumbling block for a business trying to respond quickly to an emerging situation. Hence, there is a drive to converge the disparate IT components and services within traditional IT infrastructure to enable making changes more agile and efficient.

Converged/ Hyper-converged Infrastructure

- First generation converged solutions typically converged
    - storage and compute servers or
    - network and storage layers
- Hyper-converged infrastructure software implementation
    - is built into the hyper-visor layer itself or
    - a layer on top of standard hypervisors
- Consolidates multiple infrastructure resources into a single elastic stack of x86 servers

Many flavors of converged infrastructure solutions are available in the market. The first generation solutions typically converge storage and compute servers or network and storage layers bringing in a wave of adaption in the enterprise and setting the stage for next generation convergence referred to as hyper-convergence or hyper-converged infrastructure. The name reflects the fact that many hyper-converged infrastructure software implementation is built into the hypervisor layer itself or as a layer on top of the standard

hypervisors which then consolidates multiple infrastructure resources into a single stack running on an elastic pool of x86 resources.
Hyper-converged Infrastructure
- The hyper-converged infrastructure offerings in the market takes one of two forms,
    - As a reference architecture
    - As a pre-fabricated appliance
- Hyper-convergence products and architectures consolidate many services
    - Data de-duplication
    - Data backup and replication
    - SSD cache arrays
    - WAN optimization
    - Public-cloud gateways etc.
- Combine all of these with vastly simplified management

The hyper-converged infrastructure offerings in the market takes one of the two forms: as a reference architecture, which is pretested and validated based on a flexible list of hardware and software components from multiple vendors, as a prefabricated appliance with accompanying software. Some of the leading hyper-convergence products and architectures consolidate much more than traditional compute network and storage resources and integrates many services into the fold such as data deduplication, data backup and replication, SSD cache arrays, WAN optimizations, public cloud gateways, et cetera, and they combine all of these with vastly simplified management of these infrastructure from a single pane of glass. These

technologies set the stage for next evolution of IT infrastructure referred to as software-defined data center.
Software Defined Data Center (SDDC)

- Abstraction, pooling, and policy-driven automation of most resources
- SDDC is hyper-convergence combined with policy driven automation
- SDDC enables the IT as a service (ITaaS) model within the enterprise data center
- Moving away from static, over-provisioned, inflexible and siloed infrastructure
- Towards automated, orchestrated resources optimized to business demands
- VCE, NetApp, HP, Dell, IBM, Simplivity and Nutanix are major vendors

Essentially, SDDC extends the virtualization principles of abstraction, pooling, and policy-driven automation and management to almost all of the data center resources that then enables the IT as a service model within the enterprise data center. The goal of SDDC is to move data centers away from legacy infrastructure which are static, over-provisioned, inflexible, and siloed into an automated, orchestrated set of resources to be made available on demand according to consumption patterns and policies with the view to enabling business agility. Many converged infrastructure vendors also offer SDDC solutions. Major vendors among them are VCE, which is a joint venture between VMWare, Cisco and EMC, NetApp, HP, Dell, IBM, SimpliVity, and Nutanix.

Are Enterprises Moving To Cloud?

- Enterprises are already in a big way embracing cloud
- They are reaping the economies of scale offered by the public cloud providers

- They are not willing to entirely move
  their IT infrastructure into the public
  cloud
- Virtualization, convergence and SDDC
  enables the possibility of extending the
  elasticity of the cloud to the enterprise
  data centre seamlessly – Hybrid cloud

While enterprises are already in a big way embracing and adopting the seemingly unbounded capabilities offered by various public cloud service providers and they are reaping the benefits from the economies of scale offered by the public cloud, the common observation is that they're not willing to entirely move their IT infrastructure into the public cloud although there is a desire to leverage cloud scale infrastructure where it makes sense. The advancements in virtualization, convergence, and software defined data center technologies that we discussed so far enables the possibility of extending the elasticity of the cloud to the data center seamlessly through what is referred to as a hybrid cloud model which we will be covering in detail in the next module. That then brings us to the end of the current module. And to sum up, we covered the five major building blocks of enterprise IT infrastructure which are the data centers, servers, storage, network, and end-user computing. We then looked at how virtualization, converged infrastructure, and hybrid cloud computing are enabling web-scale IT to better cater to the needs of business agility.

Moule:7 Other Enterprise Architecture Domains

Introduction and Cloud Computing

The earlier modules, that is modules three to six, explore the major enterprise architecture domains. In this current module, we will cover certain newer technology driven domains.
Focus of This Module

- Cloud Computing
- Big Data
- Enterprise Social
- Security Architecture

Specifically, this module will cover, very quickly, the following technology domains and how enterprise architecture should play a role in their adoption within the enterprise: cloud computing, big data, enterprise social technologies, and security architecture. Let's begin this exploration with cloud technologies. Enterprises often turn to cloud in search of agility and flexibility which they lack or only have limited access to when using their own IT infrastructure.

- Enterprises need the capability to experiment, innovate and be nimble to leverage opportunities and neutralize threats
- Impetus is on solving business problems effectively, quickly and economically

- Cloud technologies in various forms makes this a possibility for enterprises

In a fast paced competitive global environment where business landscape is constantly changing driven by many different factors, enterprises need to foster the capability to experiment, innovate, and be nimble to leverage opportunities, and to neutralize threats in the marketplace. The impetus is increasingly on solving business problems effectively, quickly, and economically rather than being bogged down in the rigmarole of building and managing complex IT infrastructure and services. Cloud technologies in various forms makes this a possibility for enterprises. Now let's define what cloud computing is all about.

Cloud Computing

- It is a model for enabling ubiquitous, convenient, on-demand network access to a shared pool of configurable computing resources that can be rapidly provisioned and released with minimal management effort or service provider interaction

According to National Institute of Standards and Technologies within U. S. Department of Commerce, cloud computing is a model for enabling ubiquitous, convenient, on-demand network access to a shared pool of configurable computing resources that can be rapidly provisioned and released with minimal management effort or service provider interaction. The computing resources that we're talking about here could be, for example, networks, servers, storage, applications, services, and so forth.

5 Essential Characteristics of Cloud

- On-demand Self Service

- Consumers should be able to unilaterally provision computing capabilities without human interaction with service provider
- Broad Network Access
  - Computing capabilities are exposed on the network access and accessible through heterogeneous platforms
- Resource Pooling
  - Provider's computing resources are pooled using a multi-tenant model
- Rapid Elasticity
  - Resources can be elastically scaled up and down on demand
- Measured Service
  - Cloud systems automatically monitor, control and optimize resource usage by leveraging a metering capability

NIST goes on to further qualify its definition of cloud computing using these five essential characteristics. On-demand self service, or in other words, a consumer should be able to unilaterally provision computing capabilities, such as server time and network storage as needed automatically without requiring human interaction with the

service provider. Broad network access. Capabilities are exposed over the network and accessible through standard mechanisms that promote use of the heterogeneous thin or thick client platforms and devices. Resource pooling. That is the provider's computing resources are pooled using multi-tenant model with different physical and virtual resources dynamically assigned and reassigned according to the consumer's demand. Rapid elasticity. That is resources can be elastically scaled upwards and downwards automatically based on demand. To a cloud consumer, this offers the illusion of unlimited resources available to them to be provisioned and released as needed. Measured service. That is cloud systems automatically monitor, control, and optimize resource usage by leveraging a metering capability at some level of abstraction appropriate to the type of service therefore enabling the provider to transparently report resource usage to consumers across various service offerings. Having covered the definition of cloud, it is important to grasp the idea of cloud service and deployment models. Cloud service models define the level of abstraction and control offered by the cloud platform to the consumer, and the deployment models define who the provider of the service is.

Cloud Service Models

- Software as a Service (SaaS)
- Platform as a Service (PaaS)
- Infrastructure as a Service (SaaS)

Essentially, there are three cloud service models that are most common in the industry, which are Software as a Service, Platform as a Service, and Infrastructure as a Service where the Software as a Service offers consumers the capability to use the provider's applications running on a cloud infrastructure.

- Service provider's applications run on a cloud infrastructure
- Applications accessible from various client devices thin client or API
- Consumer does not manage or control the underlying cloud infrastructure, platform or application capabilities

The applications are accessible from various client devices through either a thin client interface such as web browser or an API. With the possible exception of limited user specific application configuration settings, consumer does not manage or control the underlying cloud infrastructure, the platform, or even the individual application capabilities.

- Customer applications can be deployed on cloud infrastructure
- Consumer applications must use supported language, library, services etc.
- Consumer does not control the underlying cloud platform, but controls deployed applications

In the case of Platform as a Service model, the consumer is able to deploy customer applications onto the cloud infrastructure as long as these applications are created using the language, library, services, and tools offered by the service provider. The consumer does not control the underlying cloud infrastructure, server, storage, networking, etc., but has control over the deployed applications and in most cases the configuration settings for application's hosting environment.

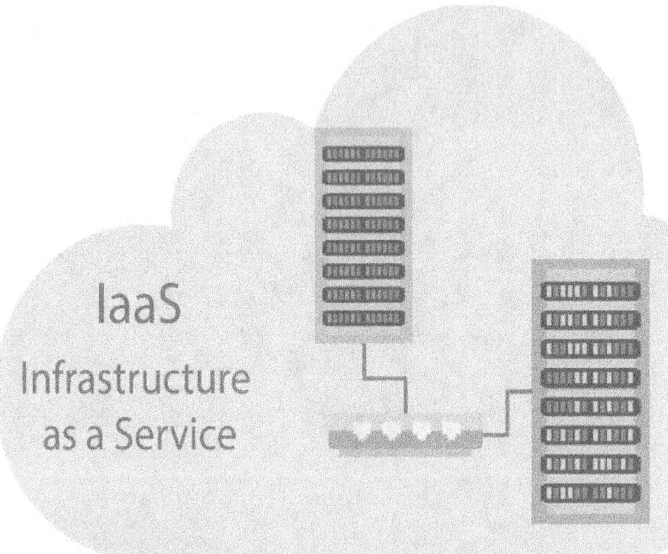

- This model offers maximum control to the cloud consumers Consumer is able to provision processing, storage, networks etc.
- Consumers can also deploy and run arbitrary software on their allocated infrastructure
- Consumers controls the OS, storage, applications and some networking components

The Infrastructure as a Service model offers maximum control to the cloud consumers. In this model, the consumer is able to provision processing, storage, networks, and other fundamental computing resources, as well as deploy and run arbitrary software. The consumer does not manage or control the underlying cloud infrastructure, but has control over the operating systems, storage, deployed applications, and select networking components.

Cloud Deployment Models

- Private
- Community

- Public
- Hybrid

The most prevalent deployment models for the cloud are private, community, public, and hybrid.

Private Cloud

- The cloud infrastructure is provisioned for exclusive use by a single organization
- It can be owned, managed or operated by the organization themselves and/or a third party
- The cloud infrastructure can be located on premise or off-premise

Private refers to the deployment model where the cloud infrastructure is provisioned for exclusive use by a single organization. It can, however, be owned, managed, or operated by either the organization's IT department playing the role of an internal service provider, or a third party playing a similar role for the organization, or a combination of both. The cloud infrastructure may itself be located on or off premise.

Community Cloud

- The cloud infrastructure is shared by a community or a collective of organizations
- A secure cloud infrastructure built exclusively for and shared by a collective of government agencies is a good example

The community cloud refers to the deployment model where the cloud infrastructure is shared by a community or a collective of organizations, which share a common interest. For example, a secure cloud infrastructure built for a collection of government agencies of a country or a state government could qualify as an example of community cloud.

Public Cloud
- Public cloud refers to a cloud infrastructure that is provisioned for use by general public

Hybrid Cloud
- Hybrid cloud refers to some combination of two or more of the private, public and community cloud infrastructure

Public cloud refers to the cloud infrastructure that is provisioned for open use by general public while hybrid cloud refers to some combination of two or more of the private, public, and community cloud infrastructure models.

EA & Enterprise Cloud Strategy
- EA takes a holistic and strategic view of enterprise's needs and opportunities
- EA can aid in road mapping the enterprise's cloud adoption journey
- Early cloud initiatives tend to be opportunistic
- Point solutions from early adoption efforts need to be harmonized through an enterprise cloud strategy

Enterprise architecture could be effectively used to leverage cloud technologies for the enterprise and to maximize its potential. Enterprise architecture typically takes a holistic and strategic view of opportunities presented by cloud technologies and hence are able to recommend a roadmap that supports a systematic adoption and rollout of these technologies across the enterprise portfolios. Most early cloud initiatives within the enterprise tend to be focused on the needs of specific project or program of work. In some cases, business units tend to even entirely bypass IT to engage external Software as a Service vendor in order to tackle urgent business problems. However, the proliferation of these point solutions could create more confusion and chaos in the long run. It is important to use a strategic roadmap to harmonize the enterprise's cloud initiatives.

Big Data

Big data is another of the exploding new fields that enterprises need to strategize and harmonize in order to extract best business value outcomes and competitive differentiation. Here are some interesting and novel applications of big data. Macy's Inc. uses big data to adjust pricing in near real time for nearly 73 million items that it sells based on demand and inventory. Walmart stores uses semantic data in its search platform and relies on text analysis, machine learning, and even synonym mining to produce relevant search results. The fast food company, McDonald's, is training their cameras on the drive through lanes to determine how long the queue is and modifies what it displays on the menu. Long queues cause the menu to present items that can be served quickly. Los Angeles Police Department uses crimes prediction software from a company called PredPol to predict where the crimes are likely to occur down to an area of 500 square meters and reports a 33% reduction of burglaries and 21% reduction in violent crimes based on these predictions. Tesco collects nearly 70, 000 refrigeration data points to keep tabs on the performance of its

refrigeration systems to gauge when machines might need to be maintained and to engage in proactive maintenance to cut its energy cost.
Three Vs of Big Data
- Volume
- Velocity
- Variety

In a nutshell, the problem that big data domain deals with involves either large volumes of data, or high velocity of data flows, or data from a variety of sources held in variety of formats, or a combination of these usually referred to as the 3Vs of big data. While it refers to the domain of data sets exhibiting these qualities,

- The term big data refers to the nature of data set as well as to the interpretive process used to churn through it
- Through this process hidden trends, patterns and links are revealed through careful analysis
- Traditional data warehousing tools are considered inadequate for this kind of analysis

the term big data usually includes the interpretive process that is used to churn through this data set to produce valuable business insights that drive business decisions and outcomes. This interpretive analysis requires unearthing hidden trends, patterns, and links by carefully analyzing the big data set. Traditional data warehousing and analytical processing tools are considered inadequate for this type of analysis. Apache Hadoop is a pioneering, open-source software that is most often associated with big data. The other alternators include products from Cloudera, Hortonworks, Amazon, Google, Microsoft, etc.
Map / Reduce

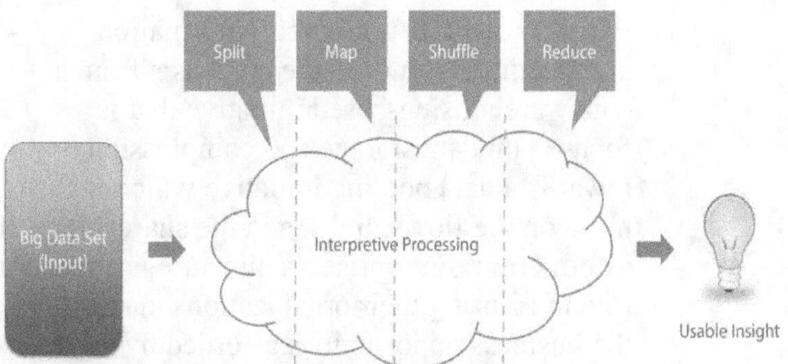

At a high level, the technology involves distributor storage and processing of data coordinated by a set of tasks known as MapReduce which then also breaks down the results into manageable chunks in order to provide summarized insights.

Key Role

- Data Scientist having deep computing background combined with expertise in mathematical and statistical analysis of data as well as expertise in an industry/domain

The key role that is responsible for defining big data solutions is the big data scientist who typically have deep computing background combined with expertise in mathematical and statistical analysis of data, as well as domain expertise in a given industry.

- Big data disrupts traditional Enterprise Information Architecture (EIA)
- Transitioning from an initiative based focused on data warehousing to data pooling
- EA has a major role to maximize business opportunities afforded by big data
- Enterprise Architects are best placed to influence a data-savvy business strategy that exploits big data

Big data disrupts traditional information architectures. It moves the emphasis from a data warehousing-based initiative that is focused on data storage and compression towards a data pooling initiative which focuses more on the flows, links, and the shareability of information. Enterprise architecture has a major role in insuring their organizations maximize the business opportunities afforded by big data technologies. Enterprises can gain best from big data opportunity by devising a data-savvy business strategy, and enterprise architects are best placed to proactively influence the direction of the strategic change by designing business outcomes that exploit big data opportunities inside and outside the organization.

Enterprise Social Technologies

Use of social technologies within the enterprise is on the rise. The term enterprise social technologies refers to a wide range of applications that enable various forms of people-to-people connectivity both within and outside the enterprise.
Enterprise Social Technologies
- Collaboration tools
- Activity streams
- Workspaces Community tools
- Social listening tools
- Social advocacy tools
- Social dashboards
- Social intelligence mining tools

These typically take the form of collaboration tools, activity streams, workspaces, community tools, social listening tools, social advocacy tools, social dashboards, social intelligence mining tools, and so forth.

- Social enterprise applications typically get deployed as point solutions tackling local problems
- These technologies tend to gain unequal uptake across the enterprise thus not realizing their potential
- Enterprise architecture is well positioned to
  - Take an integrated and holistic view of the enterprise's need for social technologies
  - Strategize, prioritize and create an enterprise social roadmap

Most often, these different applications are deployed as point solutions resulting from initiatives that are not necessarily based on a consistent and coherent enterprise-wide social strategy. Often, these technologies find unequal uptake within various business units. For instance, you may find greater uptake in marketing department while manufacturing and R&D business units, for example, may lag behind in its adoption, or vice versa. Enterprise architecture is well positioned to take an integrated and holistic view of the enterprise's need of social technologies, as well as to strategize and prioritize and create a roadmap for its uptake in order develop best value out of these technologies.

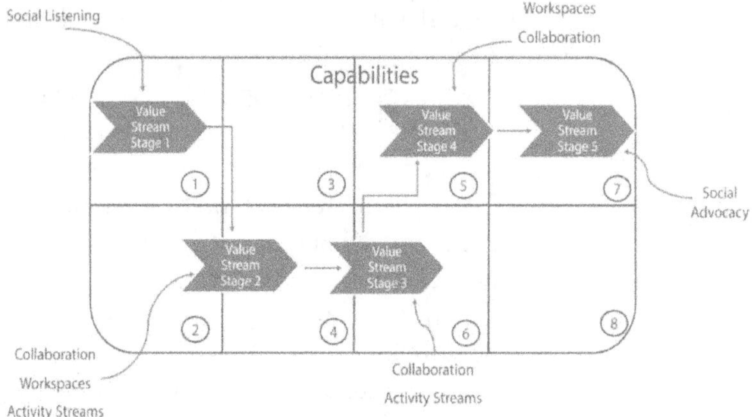

- Obtaining a holistic view of enterprise social needs.

This is typically done beginning with business architecture artifacts such as capability maps, value stream maps, etc. and overlaying enterprise social technologies and applications over this map to identify enterprise-wide social strategy. This kind of exercise would enable enterprise architecture to take a holistic view of the enterprise's social application needs and therefore enable it to create a roadmap that realizes these strategies. Yammer, Lync, Office 365 from Microsoft, Connections Suite of products from IBM, Salesforce. com, Chatter and communities, JiveX and Producteev from Jive Software, Hootsuite, Sprout Social, and SocialFlow, which provide predominantly social dashboard services, are some of the dominant products that offer services in this space.

Security Architecture

Enterprise Information Security Architecture

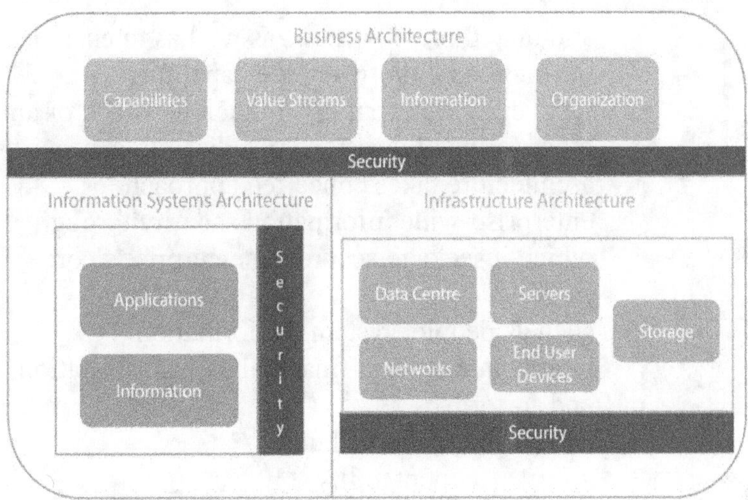

Security Architecture refers to that strand of Enterprise Architecture which focus's on securing Enterprise information assets, and it cuts across all architecture domains discussed so far. It is important to clarify at this point the phrases security architecture and enterprise security architecture are used interchangeably in this module, and

they both essentially imply the enterprise information security architecture discipline.

Goals of Security Architecture

- Protect enterprise systems and information assets from,
  - Tampering
  - Destruction
  - Unauthorized Access
- And to ensure,
  - Business Continuity
  - Recovery
- Security architecture takes a concerted approach to protecting enterprise core assets

The central goal of this strand of enterprise architecture is to protect enterprise systems and information assets from tampering, destruction,

and unauthorized access, as well as to ensure business continuity and the capability to recover in the event of a malicious attack or any other forms of disaster. As a discipline, security architecture takes concerted approach to enterprise-wide information security through which it seeks to secure the enterprise's core assets
such as people, systems, information, intellectual capital, financial assets, reputation, and so forth.
Seven Security Attributes
- Accountability
- Authentication
- Access Control
- Availability
- Confidentiality
- Integrity
- Safety

Essentially, security architecture constructs its enterprise security model through seven high level concepts, which are commonly referred to as the security attributes. Let's have a look at these attributes now. Accountability, which is, the ability to associate an activity to an actor where an actor, for example, can be a person or an automated process. This is usually enforced through mechanisms such as identity management, audit, etc. The extent to which accountability is enforced conveys the non-reputability of transactions. Authentication, which is the ability to bind an identity
to an actor through a process such as a sign on or through swiping of a security access card, for example. Access control, which determines the authenticated actor's ability to act at any given point in time within the system given a host of factors that might influence this. It is often confused with authorization which is a form of

access control based on the actor's identity alone. However, access control is wider in its implications and takes into account factors such as the time of day, the IP address, device accessed from, etc. Availability of a system, or information asset, refers to the extent of which it is functional and accessible under various circumstances. From a security architecture point of view, the main emphasis is around the ability to keep the business functions running as close to normal levels of functionality even in the event of a malicious attack or disaster and the ability to recover back to normal operations as quickly as possible. Confidentiality. This refers to preventing unintended disclosure of information to unauthorized actors and is closely related to privacy. Integrity. This refers to the ability to avoid unintended modification of data accidentally or through a malicious attack. Safety refers to the prevention of damage and injury to people, which include customers, employees, suppliers, partners, etc. Security Enforcement Mechanisms

- Planning
- Prevention
- Detection
- Diligence
- Response

The enterprise-wide initiatives and measures associated with protecting security attributes of business assets at all levels of organization are referred to as security enforcement mechanisms, and these enforcement mechanisms are often categorized along the following high-level topics: planning, prevention, detection, diligence, and response

Planning

- All forward looking functions that are aimed at proactively securing enterprise assets
- This typically involves:
    - Knowing which business assets need to be protected
    - Knowing what business drivers need to be enabled
    - Identifying and prioritizing threats
    - Identifying countermeasures
    - Identifying inter-relationships

where planning refers to the forward- looking functions that are aimed at proactively securing the enterprise assets. This typically involves understanding which business assets needs to be protected and what business drivers need to be enabled and supported; identifying threats, prioritizing these threats based on factors such as the extent of potential business impact, cost of mitigating the threat, likeliness of its occurrence, etc. ; identifying countermeasures that mitigate and nullify these threats in the order of priority, as well as identifying the interrelationship across multiple initiators and security enforcement mechanisms that are in place.

Prevention
- Refers to preventative mechanisms that protect the security attributes of the enterprise
- For Example:
    - Swipe-card access control systems
    - Security personnel
    - Network firewalls
    - Other perimeter defence systems

Prevention refers to the actual preventative mechanisms that are put in place to protect the security attributes of the enterprise. Swipe-card access control systems, security personnel, network firewalls, and other perimeter defenses are examples of the preventative function.

Detection

- Refers to security surveillance, monitoring, threat and attack detection and identification mechanisms
- For Example:
  - Fire and smoke detection systems
  - Motion detection systems
  - Security cameras
  - Network intrusion detection systems etc.

Detection refers to the security surveillance, monitoring, threat and attack detection, and identification mechanisms that are put in place to secure business assets. These mechanisms could range from fire and smoke detection, motion detection, security cameras to network intrusion detection, anti-ware, software, etc.

Response

- Refers to the ability to take quick and effective action in the event of a security breach or compromise
- This might include:
  - Enforcing isolation/ lock-down mode to contain and eradicate attacks
  - Ability to activate disaster recovery mechanisms
  - Forensics leading to enforcing strategic and tactical measures
  - Engaging effectively with law enforcement agencies

Response refers to the ability to take quick and effective action in the event of a security breach or compromise in order to limit damage and eradicate threats. This might include enforcing an isolation or lock-down mode for servers and network segments for containment and eradication of threats, ability to activate disaster recovery mechanisms, forensics to learn effectively from the incident, and enforce tactical and strategic measures, as well as to engage effectively with law enforcement authorities of the state.

Diligence

- Refers to proactive measures taken to continuously improve security architecture, such as by
    - Performing continuous vulnerability assessments
    - Reviews of internal and external processes Procedures and threat re-classifications
- The intent is to continuously evolve the enterprise's security stance

Diligence refers to the proactive measures taken on a continual basis to improve security architecture, such as by performing continuous vulnerability assessments, review of internal and external processes and procedures, and threat classifications taking into account new disruptive changes in business and technology landscapes, government regulations, etc. The intent of these measures overall is to continuously evolve the organization's security stance with the changing internal and external security needs of the enterprise. Modern enterprises are in a state of constant flux. New technologies, business initiatives, expansions, regulatory regimes all have security implications for the enterprise.

- Security architecture enables enterprises to take a holistic perspective on the security needs of the organization

- Security architecture frameworks provide a structured way of thinking about enterprise security
- Popular among these include
  - SABSA (Sherwood Applied Business Security Architecture)
  - ISO 27001
  - Open Security Architecture
  - COBIT
  - ITIL V3
  - NIST 800-53 etc.

Security architecture enables enterprises to take a holistic perspective on the security needs of the organization rather than being drowned in the day-to-day operational concerns that are focused around incident responses, compliance reviews, and security audits. Security architecture frameworks provide a structured way of thinking about enterprise security. Popular among these include SABSA, which stands for Sherwood Applied Business Security Architecture, ISO 27001, and Open Security Architecture. There are also other more elaborate frameworks and standards followed in the industry which covers not only architecture, but also implementation, operations, and ongoing maintenance of enterprise information security. Some of these include COBIT, ITIL V3, NIST 800-53. That brings us to the end of the current module which provided a quick overview of some of the miscellaneous architecture areas that were not dealt with in the earlier modules. Just to recap very quickly, this module covered Cloud Architecture, Big Data Architecture, Enterprise Social, and Security Architecture.

Module:8 Architect Roles in Enterprise

Introduction

In this module, we will talk about the various architectural roles within the enterprise. Before we begin the exploration of the various roles, it is important to recognize that enterprises come in many shapes and sizes. There are considerable variations across the industry in terms of the value they produce and the services they provide. These variations are naturally reflected on how they are structured and organized. The architecture roles of the enterprise hence are influenced by what an enterprise actually does. Also, it is important to keep in mind that the enterprise architecture as a discipline and practice has been around for more than three decades. Developed in the 70s and pioneered by many in the 80s and 90s and re-emerged in the 2000s, it's undergoing considerable transformation at the present times. Many organizations tend to have a lot of legacy attached to the practice mingled with some forward thinking and forward-looking changes brought about by the need to stay relevant in a fast-changing environment. If you consider the architects working on physical structures such as a house or a small building, they may work with different sets of concerns, concepts, and patterns than an architect working on a large skyscraper. And again, the concerns,

concepts, patterns, and design framework that these architects are interested in
is in turn different from that of say the urban designer or planners. This is similar for the architect roles within the enterprise as well. Each role works at different levels of abstraction. Some typical architectural roles in an enterprise are listed here.

Typical Architecture Roles in Enterprise

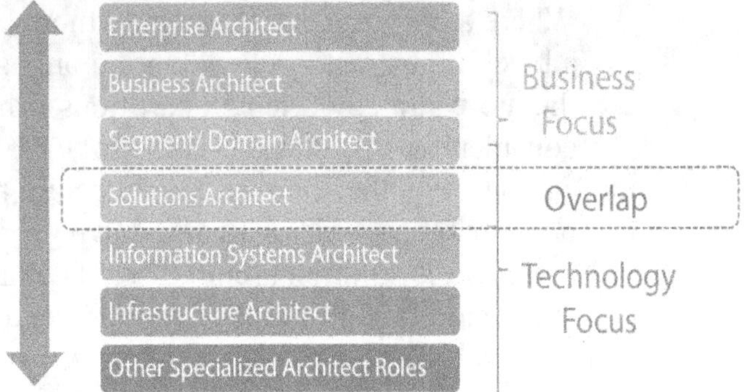

As indicated, some of these roles tend to have strategic orientation while other have more implementation orientation. Some roles have business focus while others have technology focus, and some roles tend to have a blended focus shared between business and technology. The diagram shown here is from FEAF, which stands for Federal Enterprise Architecture Framework, and it shows the variation among the architecture partitions across four different dimensions.

Enterprise Architecture Roles - FEAF

Level	Scope	Detail	Impact	Audience
Enterprise Architecture	Agency/ Organization	Low	Strategic Outcomes	All Stakeholders
Segment Architecture	Line of Business	Medium	Business Outcomes	Business Owners
Solution Architecture	Function/ Process	High	Operational Outcomes	Users and Developers

Where a partition can be roughly thought of as a level of abstraction, the diagram only shows the more strategy oriented partitions, which are considered as EA roles by the FEAF. As you can observe, the enterprise architecture has a broader scope which narrows down gradually towards the solution architecture. The impact dimension tend to follow a similar trend while the level of detail these architectural partitions focus tend to follow an opposite trend.
Enterprise Architecture Roles - TOGAF

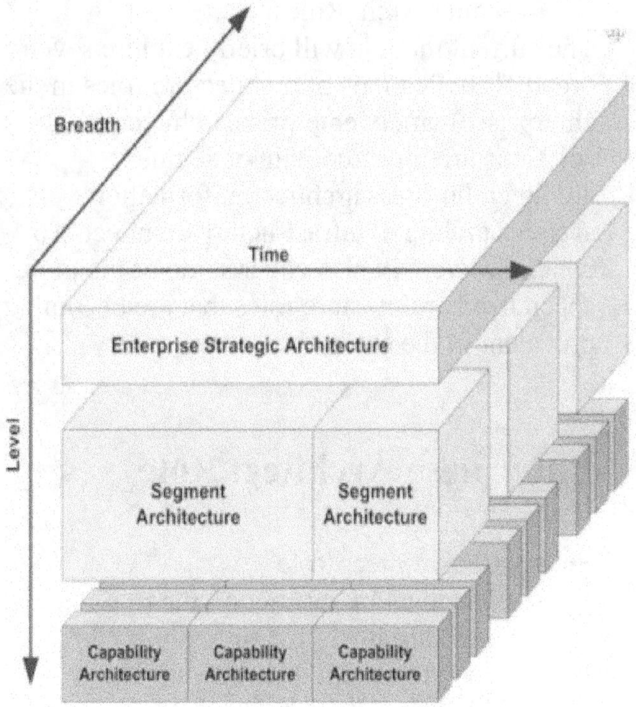

TOGAF conveys a similar idea about the architecture partitions using a slightly different diagram. Notice how the bottom-most partition is comprised of smaller building blocks and are referred to as capability architecture. A number of capabilities can be grouped under a single architecture block of the segment partition, and the segment blocks are in turn integrated by the enterprise architecture partition. In this module, we will dig a little deeper into the roles of architects functioning at different layers of abstractions.

Focus of this module
- Enterprise Architect
- Solutions Architect
- Domain or Segment Architect
- Business Architect
- Information Systems Architect
- Infrastructure Architect

- Other Arch. Roles

The current module will briefly explore seven broad classifications of architecture roles in the enterprise, namely enterprise architect, solutions architect, domain or segment architect, business architect, information systems architect, infrastructure architect. To conclude, we will also cover some of the more specialized architecture roles that are becoming prevalent in the enterprise scene.

Enterprise Architect Role

Enterprise Architect Role
- The level of abstraction the role operates at
- The value add, in terms of:
    - Goals & Tasks
    - Interactions
    - Artefacts

So let's explore the enterprise architect role in some detail. In this video, we will attempt to define the role from the following perspectives: the level of detail or abstraction at which the role operates, how the role adds value from the point of view of the goals and tasks performed by the role, who they interact with, as well as the artifacts produced in the book of their work. Let's begin by understanding the level of abstraction or detail at which the role operates.
Enterprise -wide
- Mission
- Values
- Vision
- Strategy

Scope is the entire enterprise
- Business

- Technology capabilities
- Other capabilities
- Operations
- Value chains
- External entities

Comprehends the enterprise

- Business models
- Operating models
- Capabilities, processes, value chains & value streams
- Organizational structure
- Portfolios of initiatives
- How they overlap & interconnect
- Architecture principles
- Patterns & anti -patterns
- Good & best practices
- Current and target states

An enterprise architect thinks at the level of enterprise-wide mission, values, vision, and strategy. The emphasis of the role is predominantly focused on strategy formulation and ensuring its effective execution across the enterprise. The scope of the EA's role spans the entire enterprise, the business, the technology capabilities, supporting the business, the production and manufacturing capabilities, the operations and its day-to-day management, the organization's value chains, the external third parties such as vendors, service providers, partners, industry bodies, legal and regulatory teams it's operating within. The EA comprehends the enterprise through abstractions such as enterprise business model, its operating models, its capabilities, processes, value chains and value streams, as well as organizational structure and their geographic distribution, portfolio of initiatives, and the applications, technology, and information supporting the overall business. It also

maintains an understanding of how all these overlap and interconnect. And finally, EA role also concerns itself with the principles, patterns, anti-patterns, the good and best practices, the current state of the enterprise, the envisioned target state, and the road map for transition. Now that we have a general sense of the abstraction and scope at which the role operates,
let's now explore how the role adds value. We will begin by exploring what goals the role operate with and what kinds of tasks it performs.
Goals
- Inform/ Influence and support strategy formulation
- Architecture vision for the target state
- Capture the current state of the enterprise's architecture
- Formulate and evolve high-level architecture roadmap
- Architectural agility through agile processes and building blocks
- Business and technology innovations

One of the key goals of the enterprise architect role is to effectively inform, influence, and support the formulation of the overall business strategy, as well as to create and evolve the architectural vision for a target state enterprise, which is in alignment with the business strategy. The enterprise architect also captures the current state of the enterprise through various architectural perspectives and viewpoints. They also formulate and evolve the high-level architectural roadmaps to realize the vision through various enterprise initiatives. The roadmap, by the way, forms the key component of the architectural strategy for the

enterprise. In addition to these traditional goals, the
new demands on this role also includes goals such as to build and operate an agile architectural process, as well as to create architectural building blocks that are agile and nimble to enable, support, and foster business and technical innovations. Module nine deals with the last two goals of the enterprise architect role in greater detail.
Interacts With
- CXOs, heads of business units
- Domain/ Subject-matter experts
- Segment, solution, business, applications, data, technology, security architects
- Vendors and service providers
- Partners and customers
- Industry bodies and regulatory authorities

The role typically interacts and consults for the senior executives and heads of business units to help create and evolve strategies. The role also works with subject matter experts, also referred to as domain experts, to understand the problem domain and the business objectives more closely. The role interacts with other architects who are closer to the problem domain and the capabilities, such as the
segment and solution architects, as well as infrastructure applications and security architects. The role interacts with vendors and service providers and industry analysts to stay on top of the technology trends and the various service offerings in the marketplace. It also maintains relationships with various partners and customers or customer impersonators within the organization to understand the key pain points, desires, and aspirations in their

relationship with the enterprise. It also is connected to industry bodies and regulatory authorities to stay on top of the changes that the organization need to be prepared for.

Artefacts

- Architecture is not all about artefacts
- Artefacts aids and supports but do not substitute interaction and communication
- Uses a variety of artefacts as appropriate and relevant for the consumers, not limited to Capability, strategy, process and organization maps
- Architectural vision, baseline and target state architectures and architecture roadmaps
- Reference architectures, standards, principles, policies and process guidelines

The general guidance for modern enterprise architecture practice is not to be artifact happy, or, in other words, to not think about architecture work only in terms of producing documents and artifacts. Here teams produce various high-level architectural artifacts as an appropriate and relevant for stakeholders and consumers in general including capability maps, strategy maps, process maps, organization maps; architectural vision typically spanning three to five years horizon and sometimes even longer in the case of some foundational infrastructure; baseline and target state architecture across business applications, information, and infrastructure domains typically at a conceptual and logical level of abstractions; architecture roadmaps, which is an enterprise initiatives-based view of how the envision target state architecture can be achieved. Enterprise architects are also responsible for reference architectures, standards, principles, policies, and process guidelines. That completes the overview of the enterprise architect role.

Solutions Architect Role

Solutions Architect Role
- The level of abstraction the role operates at
- The value the role brings to the table
  - Goals & Tasks
  - Interactions
  - Artefacts

Let's explore the solution architect role. We will use a similar pattern to what we used to explore enterprise architecture role. That is we will first try and get an understanding of the level of abstraction at which the role operates. Then we will look at how the role adds value in terms of the goals of role and the tasks performed by the role, who they typically interact with, the typical artifacts produced by the role.

Level of Abstraction
- Focuses on Enterprise Initiatives (Projects/ Programs)
  - Project/ program vision
  - Business drivers & objectives
  - Aligning to enterprise architecture vision
  - Functional, non -functional & operational requirements
  - Integrates multiple architecture perspectives
  - Constraints, assumptions, issues and risks
  - Principles, patterns and practices

So first, the level of abstraction the role operates at. The solution architect, or the SA, works at the level of specific enterprise initiatives. That is the role operates in the context of one or more projects or programs of work. The role focuses on the vision and mission of the initiatives unlike an enterprise architect whose scope is the whole of the enterprise. The solution architect identifies the key business drivers for the initiatives and seeks to fulfill the business objectives that need to be met. At the same time, the role is also responsible for understanding the architectural vision and enablement of enterprise strategy through the project initiatives. The solution architect works closely with the functional, non-functional, and operational requirements of the initiative and ensures that the created solution meet those requirements. The SA seeks to bring together application, technology, integration, data, and security architectural viewpoints
into a coherent and usable solution while operating within the constraints, framework of assumptions, issues and risk perceptions the initiative is operating under. The solution architect ensures compliance and adherence to enterprise architecture principles, patterns, and best practices within the solution space.
How Does the SA Role Add Value?
Goals

- Create effective solutions at the project and program level
- Meets business objectives set for the program
- Aligning solution architecture to enterprise and domain architecture
- Architectural governance at the initiative level

- Solicits and incorporates multiple architectural perspectives

Let's now dig deeper to understand how the role adds value. The solution architect's main goal is to create effective solutions at the project and program level that meets business objectives set for the program to ensure the architecture of the solutions developed are in alignment with the enterprise and domain architecture vision and strategies and to enable effective architectural oversight and ongoing governance while transitioning the project or program to the detailed design and implementation phases. They also seek to incorporate multiple perspectives within the solution.

Interacts With …

- Business stakeholders and domain experts
- Enterprise and segment/ domain architects
- Project, Program and Release management
- Business analysts, customer experience specialists, developers, tech. leads, testers and other architects (from domains such as infrastructure, security, application, data etc.)
- Vendors, partners, service providers and customers

Solution architect interacts with business stakeholders and domain experts to understand the problem space, the pain points, and the business vision for that solution. The role interacts with enterprise and domain architects to comprehend the evolving enterprise architectural landscape and the architectural roadmap in order to ensure architectural alignment within the solution space. The architect works alongside project or program stakeholders such as project managers, program managers, and release managers to provide ongoing clarifications and architectural support, and they also consult as needed in the project and program steering committees. The role interacts with team members in a multi-functional team to bring a solution to life. The team typically includes business analysts, customer experience specialists, developers, technical leads, domain specialists, testers, and other architects. They also interact with vendors, partners, service providers, and customers to enable crafting a solution that integrates multiple solution viewpoints into a cohesive whole.

Artefacts

- Creates solution concepts
- Early and high-level estimates
- High-level baseline architecture view of the solution

Solution architects typically create solution concepts at the commencement of an initiative. At this stage, the SA works with the key business stakeholders, enterprise architects, and project stakeholders to perform an early and very high-level analysis of the feasibility of the solution. This exercise, when undertaken, happens as part of establishing the business case for an initiative. Solutions architect may also product high level and early estimates in collaboration with project or program stakeholders. When the initiative is funded, the solution architect creates the high-level architecture document to create a baseline architecture view of the solution incorporating multiple perspectives as appropriate and relevant to the stakeholders involved. This document typically also includes a framework of assumptions, issues, and risks involved, as well as captures dependencies on other enterprise initiatives. That completes the overview of the solution architect role.

Segment or Domain Architect Role

Lets Focus On ...
- Enterprise Architect
- Solutions Architect
- **Domain or Segment Architect**
- Business Architect
- Information Systems Architect
- Infrastructure Architect
- Other Arch. Roles

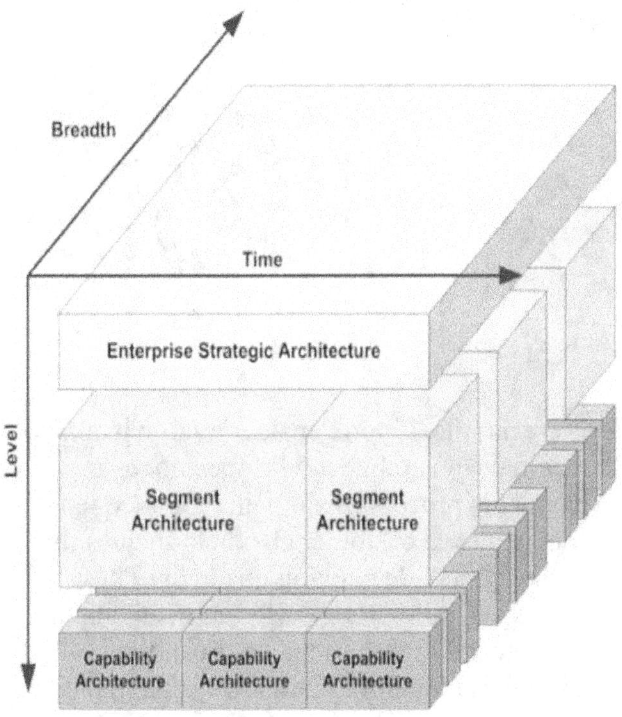

Let's now look at the segment or domain
architecture role in greater detail. As discussed
earlier in the module, the segment partition
represents the layer of abstraction that is
between the enterprise architecture and
capability architecture layers. The capability
architecture generally refers to the level three
capability layer in a
capability map and can therefore be roughly
equated to the solutions architecture layer.
However, enterprises typically don't have
designations such as segment architect, but
instead there are architects who are typically
subject matter specialists in certain business
domains or lines of businesses within the
enterprise. These are architects are usually
referred to as domain architects.
Consider a Large Bank…

For example, if you consider a large bank, you
may have an architect who specializes in
payments processing domain or someone who
specializes in customer channels such as its
online or mobile banking channels. These
architects are typically referred to as domain
architects. In our current example, these
architects may hold titles such as payments
architect, online banking architect, or mobile
banking architect.

Segment Architect Role

- Solution Architect
  - Focuses on one or more specific enterprise initiatives
- Segment Architect
  - Focus spans an entire segment or domain, usually spanning multiple capabilities
- Enterprise Architect
  - Focus spans the entire enterprise

A segment architect functions a lot like an enterprise architect; however, limiting his role to a single business domain or line of business. Many large businesses who have large portfolio of products and/or services under its umbrella prefer to group capabilities under different domains and tend to have architectural vision and road map

for each domain, which then in turn integrates into the overall vision for the enterprise. In that sense, domain architect role kind of straddles between the enterprise architect and solution architect roles. This role works closely with the solution architect role to ensure that domain-specific architecture vision and strategy is realized through the initiatives undertaken in that domain while at the same time working with the enterprise architects to ensure that the domain architecture vision is in alignment with the overall direction and strategic objectives of the enterprise.

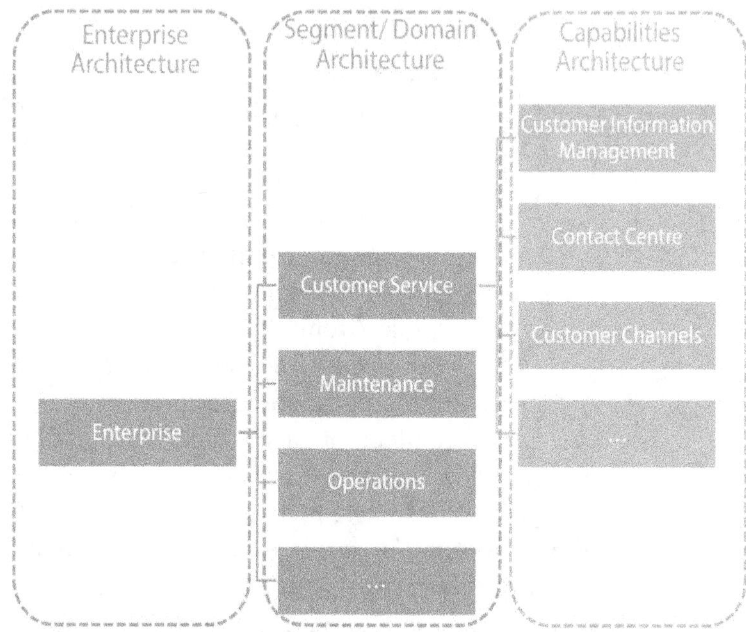

For example, a large enterprise may have multiple domains such as customer service, maintenance, operations, etc., which can be considered as business domains. Customer service, in turn, may have multiple capabilities underneath it such as customer information management, contact center, customer channels, and so forth. Each of these correspond to capabilities. While a solutions architect may work at the abstraction level of capabilities or at even smaller granular layers, the domain architect, who is typically a senior solutions architect with several years of experience in a given domain, may be designated a domain architect and function like an enterprise architect within that domain. That concludes our quick overview of the segment or domain architect role.

Business Architect Role

Lets Focus On …
- Enterprise Architect
- Solutions Architect
- Domain or Segment Architect
- **Business Architect**
- Information Systems Architect
- Infrastructure Architect
- Other Arch. Roles

Business Architect Role
- Strategic business role
- Enterprise-wide scope focusing on business domains
- Business insights without the distractions of technology
- Business architect's work impact
  - Business operating model
  - Strategy development
  - Capabilities
  - Processes
  - Value Streams etc.

Having looked at the domain architect role who specialize in business domains, let us now focus our attention to enterprise architect roles that specialize in various architectural domains. It is important to note that these domains, that is the business information systems and infrastructure domains, have been explored earlier in the module of their own each. The intent of this section therefore is to provide a quick overview of the roles operating within each of these domains. To begin with, we will look at the role of business architect. Business architect is a strategic business role, which like an enterprise architect role, typically have an enterprise-wide scope; however, focusing on business domains without necessarily crossing over or attempting to address architectural concerns of the technology domains. The role attempts to gain business insights without the distractions, overtones, and the complexities introduced by technology implementations. The business architect's work have impact on areas such as business operating models, strategy development, mapping and streamlining of capabilities, processes, value streams, etc. Typically, business architects work in the context of large enterprise initiatives that are introducing transformative changes and have implications spanning across the organization.

- Rolling out strategic changes
- Mergers and acquisitions
- New products/ services
- Globalization
- Operational streamlining
- Regulatory compliance
- Outsourcing

Some of these initiatives include rolling out strategic changes and guiding strategy implementation across the enterprise, mergers and acquisitions planning and their rollout, new products or services rollout, globalization or expanding to newer markets or market segments, operational streamlining, regulatory compliance management, identifying outsourcing opportunities, etc.

Interacts With …

- Senior executives and enterprise architects
- Business unit leads
- Subject matter experts, business analysts and domain architects

Business architects typically work with senior executives and enterprise architects to create and evolve enterprise strategy. They interact with business unit leaders to understand their pain points and strategic, as well as tactical objectives. They also work with subject matter experts, business analysts, and domain architects in the book of their work.

Artefacts

- Business architecture blueprint
- Strategy map
- Capabilities map
- Value map
- Initiatives map
- Organization map
- Services map
- Business operating models

The business architects create business architecture blueprints which help analyze how various parts of the enterprise interact and work together. It clarifies and highlights inefficiencies, redundancies, and structural and process misalignments. The business architecture blueprint also enables looking at the business from various viewpoints relevant for business stakeholders, which typically includes strategy map, capability map, value map, initiative map, organization map, services map, and business operating models, which includes the current target, as well as the transition state models. That concludes the quick overview of the business architect role.

Information Systems Architect Role

Lets Focus On …

- Enterprise Architect
- Solutions Architect

- Domain or Segment Architect
- Business Architect
- **Information Systems Architect**
- Infrastructure Architect
- Other Arch. Roles

Twin Responsibilities

Information Systems Architect has twin responsibilities:

- Enterprise Applications Architecture
- Enterprise Information Architecture

Roles are often split along these lines

We will now explore the information systems architect role. This role essentially has twin responsibilities. That is architecting enterprise applications, as well as architecting the enterprise information assets. Hence, in most enterprises, you can see the role split along these lines. First, we will look at the applications architect role followed by the information architect role. The applications collectively can be thought of as the software instances of the business capabilities and processes.

Applications Architect Role

- Applications are software instantiation of business capabilities and processes
- Focuses on the overall applications strategy
- Aims to achieve consistency and interoperability across the portfolio
- Responsible for creating and evolving reference architecture
- Applications architect shepherds and evolves enterprise APIs

Unlike an application architect who focuses on the design and implementation architecture of one or more individual applications, an enterprise applications architect, spelled with an S at the end, focuses on the overall application strategy for the organization and attempts to evolve the entire application's portfolio to align with the strategic direction and roadmap of the organization. Most applications do not require to be built on drastically different approaches or technology stacks. Inconsistency across the portfolio can increase complexity and cost. Enterprise applications architect's goal is to reduce complexity and cost by bringing in consistency and interoperability across the portfolio of applications. To meet this end, the role is responsible for creating and continually grooming the applications reference architecture. The reference architecture is a collection of enterprise-approved standard building blocks, which are usually the products, platforms, and services, as well as principles, standards, patterns, and policies used to build the enterprise applications. The applications architect, in addition to the applications portfolio, is responsible for shepherding the enterprise's portfolio of business services and microservices exposed internally and externally as its API.

Interacts With …

- Technical stakeholders of various initiatives
- Architects from other architecture and business domains

The applications architect role collaborates actively with the technical stakeholders of initiatives, which are both planned and underway, in order to harvest good principles, innovations, new technologies, patterns, and practices, which then is propagated to the entire enterprise by incorporating them into reference architecture of the enterprise. The applications architect collaborates closely with architects

focused on other enterprise architecture
domains to communicate, socialize, as well as
to validate the strategic roadmap of the
applications portfolio. While applications form
the software engines that are virtual instances of
the business capabilities and processes,
Enterprise Information Architect

- Information powers the enterprise
  software
- The role is responsible for strategic
  management and use of enterprise
  information assets

data and information in general can be viewed
as the fuel that powers and runs these engines,
like how an applications architect is responsible
for the organization's overall application
strategy.

Similarly, an enterprise information architect is
responsible for strategic management and use
of enterprise assets.

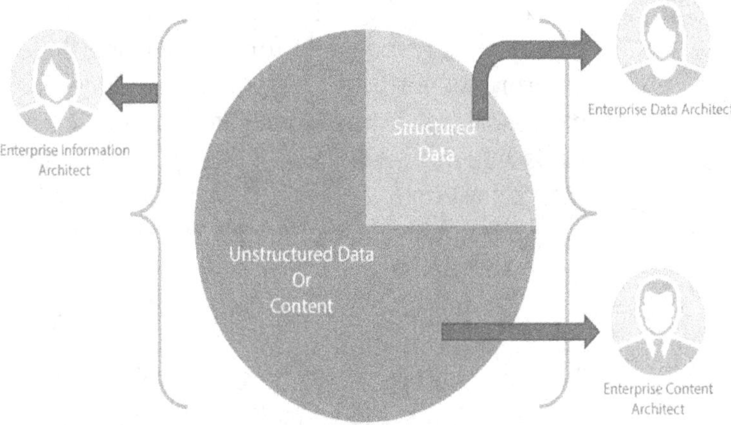

At the high level, there are two broad categories
of data at play within the enterprise, structured
Data, which is predominantly relational data,
unstructured Data or content, which refers to all
other forms of data and includes images,
documents, video, and other forms of content.
Some enterprises choose to split the roles along

those lines with the enterprise data architect
focusing on the relational data and enterprise
content architect role focusing on unstructured
data and enterprise information architect having
a broader portfolio which
includes structured, as well as other forms of
information. In this section, we will cover the
broad role of enterprise information architect.
Enterprise Information Architect

- Focuses on data/ content usage concerns
  across applications portfolio
- Seeks to unlock information assets of
  the enterprise
- Helps the enterprise to stay on top of
  their data/ information needs
- Actively maintains the inventory of data
- Model and architect information

The information architect role focuses on
implications, patterns, and concerns that apply
across multiple applications within the
portfolio. The goal of this role is to unlock the
information from the applications that produce
it so that they can be reliably and consistently
interpreted and used across the entire portfolio
of applications and treated as an enterprise
asset. The enterprise information architect helps
the enterprise stay ahead of the curve of its
evolving data and information needs. They
actively maintain the
inventory of enterprise's data and its
information assets in general, as well as model
how the information is structured, stored,
accessed, shared, archived, backed up, and
purged across multiple enterprise applications
in alignment with the strategic enterprise
architectural vision.
Interacts With …

- Enterprise applications architect

- Architects from other domains such as infrastructure, business etc.
- Technical and business stakeholders of initiatives as required

The role typically works very closely with the applications architecture team as information almost always is used in context of the applications. They also interact with architects from other domains such as infrastructure, business, etc. They interface with technical and business stakeholders of initiaives as required.
Artefacts...

- Enterprise information standards
- Taxonomies
- Metadata frameworks

The information architecture role develops enterprise information standards, taxonomies, and metadata frameworks for data and content, which unlocks the information assets to be used across the entire application's portfolio of the enterprise, as well as across organization boundaries to aid interaction through exchange of information between enterprise suppliers, partners, service providers, and customers thus enabling business agility. And that concludes our overview of the information systems architect role.

Infrastructure and Other Architect Roles

Lets Focus On ...

- Enterprise Architect
- Solutions Architect
- Domain or Segment Architect
- Business Architect

- Information Systems Architect
- **Infrastructure Architect**
- Other Arch. Roles

Infrastructure Architect

- To architect a stable and adaptable architecture
- To drive standardization and thereby reduce complexity across the building blocks

Moving on to infrastructure architect role. Technology infrastructure is the foundation that other architecture domains, such as application and information architecture, builds on. Infrastructure architects are also referred to as technology architects. The mission of an infrastructure architect is to architect a stable and adaptable architecture across the typical IT infrastructure building blocks such as data centers, servers, networking, storage, and user devices, and to work with the specialists and subject matter experts to drive standardization within each of the architecture building blocks thereby reducing complexity across these building blocks.

Infrastructure Architecture

- Strategic
  - Enable EA vison
  - Defining standards
  - Align to & evolve standards
  - Influence EA roadmap
- Tactical
  - Provisioning environments
  - Enable enterprise initiatives
  - Non -functional requirements
- Operational
  - Guidance, good and best practice
  - Catering to operational needs
  - High -level escalation points

Infrastructure architects typically have three-pronged focus, which are strategic, tactical, and operational focus areas. From a strategic view, the infrastructure architect focuses on evolving the infrastructure to enable enterprise architecture vision. Infrastructure architects play a key role to work with various domain specialists to identity and define standards and align infrastructure architecture to enterprise standards across all its building blocks. However, it is important to note that infrastructure architecture domain is dynamic, and there is a constant influx of new technologies which enable greater optimization, significant cost reductions, and present significant potential new opportunities to be leveraged by the business. Hence, the focus of infrastructure architects is not limited to complying with the enterprise architecture strategic roadmap, but they also continually inform and influence the roadmap. Provisioning and configuring environments to support new initiatives constitute its key tactical activities. Infrastructure architects are constantly in touch with key stakeholders representing enterprise initiatives to plan, design, build, configure, and support and maintain the environments for hosting enterprise systems that are built out by these initiatives. And the infrastructure architect primarily focuses on ensuring non- functional requirements of the solution are catered for at the present time and into the future while staying in alignment with the enterprise's strategic roadmap. On the operational front, the infrastructure architects focus on providing good and best practice guidance to infrastructure engineers. They also ensure that the operational needs of the enterprise systems are catered for by the architecture and design,

as well as they function as high-level escalation
point to troubleshoot infrastructure-related
issues. That concludes our overview of the
infrastructure architect role.

Lets Focus On …
- Enterprise Architect
- Solutions Architect
- Domain or Segment Architect
- Business Architect
- Information Systems Architect
- Infrastructure Architect
- **Other Arch. Roles**

Newer Technology Domains
- Mobility
- Cloud
- Unified Communication
- Enterprise Social Wearables
- Internet of Things
- Telematics
- Robotics

Key Drivers
- Greater Customer centricity
- Operational excellence
- Business innovations
- Expanded marketplace
- Expanded products and services

And finally, let's briefly discuss the ever newer
set of architecture roles that are sprouting in the
industry and the marketplace that have focus on
specific technology areas. Enterprises are
adopting new technologies at a faster clip than
ever before. Technologies such as mobility,
cloud, unified communication, enterprise social
technologies, wearables, Internet of Things,
telematics, robotics are all finding their way
into the enterprise and over time will be
incorporated into the enterprise technologies
stack. These changes are driven primarily by
the need for the organization to achieve greater

customer centricity, operational excellence, business innovations, expanded marketplace, products, service offerings, etc. As new technologies are introduced into the enterprise space, and as they reach maturity and become part of the enterprise's strategic roadmap, there needs to be a concerted effort to harvest these capabilities to drive strategic planning and execution. While the traditional architect roles are expanding and are being reconfigured to meet the new expanded needs of the enterprise, at the same time new architecture roles focusing on these new technology areas are becoming increasingly prevalent in the industry. That brings us to the end of this module.

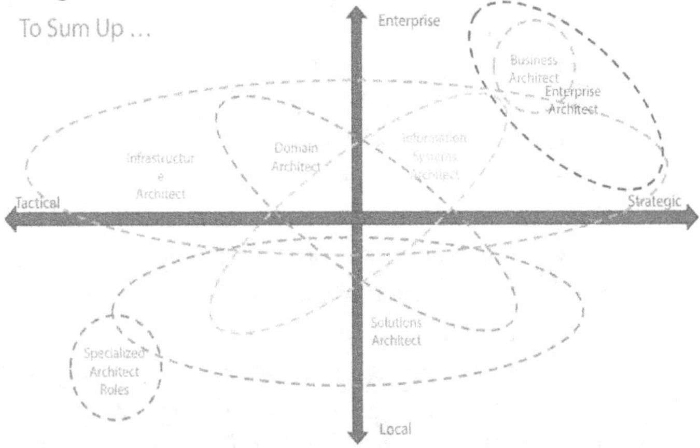

To sum up, the roles we have covered in this module can be plotted on a graph where the horizontal axis represents the tactical to strategic continuum and the vertical axis represents the impact continuum. The top representing the enterprise-wide impact, and the bottom represents local impact. Given this, based on what we have seen in this module, the enterprise architect role, which is highly strategic and tend to have broadest impact seem to operate from this zone while the solution architect with its local scope, strategic intent, and tactical and operational constraints seem to operate here. The domain or segment architect has strategic, as well as tactical scope, and tend to have broad impact, and yet it is confined to an even business domain. The business architect occupies a similar zone as the enterprise architect, but his scope excludes technology domains. The information systems architect is both strategic, as well as tactical. It tends to have a broad scope and local implications. The infrastructure architect typically has large impact. It can be tactical, as well as strategic. At the same time, it needs to accommodate some nuances required by specific solutions. Specialized architecture roles typically start their life local to a specific and tactical solution, and as it matures, moves higher in strategic and impact access.

Module:9 Agile and Enterprise Architecture

Introduction

In the recent times, the market has seen a renewed search in the eruption of lean practices, as well as, scaling agility within the enterprise. In this module, we will explore some of the rationality behind this movement and the impact this has had on enterprise architecture practice, and how to shape the practice into the future. There is a prevailing notion in the industry that agility and architecture are, by definition, antithetic. In other words, they are pulled apart in their indents and methods. Architecture development methods and frameworks, such as the one proposed by Togaf, seemed to suggest a waterfall-like approach, and hence, does not help that perception. Others, like Zachman framework, does not explicitly talk about a process for developing architecture, and hence, leaves a lot of room for interpretation.

Common Perceptions on Agile

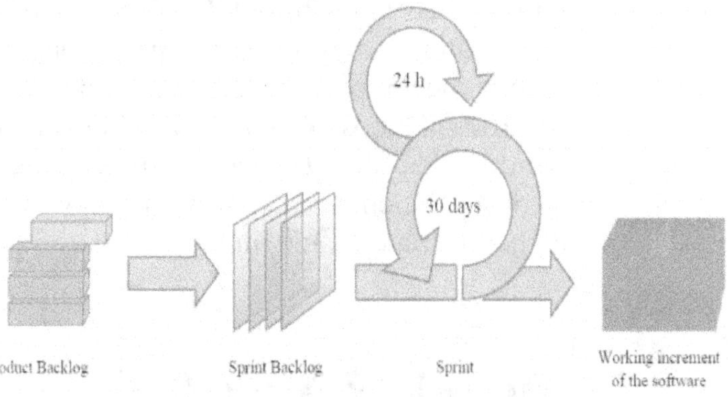

- Short iterations
- Incremental implementation
- Emergent design
- Continuous feedback and learning
- Pair programming
- Process, methodologies, frameworks and tools that support agile software development

And the common-place perception about agile is that it is all about short iterations, incremental implementation, emergent design, continuous feedback, pair programming, as well as processes, rituals, methodologies, frameworks, and tools that enables agile way of working,

hence there is discretion that prepares the room for
architecture in the agile scheme of things. In fact, it's not architecture all about big, upfront design and hence, an anti-pattern that is frowned upon by the agile camp. Well, that is only one side of the story, but there is more to it if you're willing to open to other points of view and are willing to examine agility more closely, and this is exactly what we will attempt to do in this module.

Agile & EA Compliment Each Other

- Examine Principles in Agile Manifesto
- Forces Driving Lean/ Scaled Agility
- Impact on EA Practice
- What Is Lean/ Agile Architecture?

We will examine how enterprise architecture fits into the agile scheme of things, and in fact, as you will see shortly, how they depend on and compliment each other. We will do this systematically by first examining the foundational principles intwined in the Agile Manifesto and briefly looking at reasons why it is about time to evolve these principles further along. We will look at the macro forces that is increasingly making lean and agile practices relevant, not only for the
development, operations, and support layers of the organization, but for the whole enterprise. We will look at what this means for enterprise architecture practice and where it is heading to. We will then conclude by examining what we mean by lean and agile architecture.

Examining Agile Manifesto

Agile & EA Compliment Each Other

- **Examine Principles in Agile Manifesto**
- Forces Driving Lean/ Scaled Agility
- Impact on EA Practice
- What Is Lean/ Agile Architecture?

Manifesto for Agile Software Development

- We are uncovering better ways of developing software by doing it and helping others do it.
- Through this work we have come to value:

  - Individuals and interactions over processes and tools
  - Working software over comprehensive documentation
  - Customer collaboration over contract negotiation
  - Responding to change over following a plan

- That is, while there is value in the items on the right, we value the items on the left more.

http://www.agilemanifesto.org/

Agile – Key Success Factors

- Delivering great products that customers love

  - For both internal and external customers

- Creating the right culture and environment for knowledge-work

  - Liberating software development from a "dilbert-esque" work culture

So, let's examine the agile manifesto. Agile has been around for about a decade and a half, and you may already be familiar with the agile manifesto, but let's have a quick recap. Here is what the manifesto says: we are uncovering better ways of developing software by doing it and helping others do it. Through this work, we have come to value individuals and interactions over processes and tools, working software over comprehensive documentation, customer collaboration over contract negotiation, responding to change over following a plan. That is, while there is value in the items on the right, we value
the items on the left more. It may not seem too significant in the first glance, but these simple and elegantly phrased values succinctly and beautifully captures the essence of what agile moment stands for. It has inspired a generation of software developers and created an industry moment, which we can now say has gone mainstream. In fact, the key to the success of this moment, as some of the original authors

and signatories of the manifest had with a tinge
of humor, of book, are in fact the mushy stuff;
the stuff that we, as professionals, hold close to
our heart. It is about delivering great products
to our customers, which, in the enterprise
context, may be an end consumer of the product
or service or it could be an internal stakeholder.
So, again, it is about creating the right work
environment for collaboration and knowledge-
work. That is, it's intent was to liberate software
development, and software developers in
particular, from the clutches of what the authors
of the manifesto refer to as the dilbert-esque
work culture. And there is no doubt that agile
movement has achieved these objectives in a
big way, and is today, a major influence in
changing the world culture of the software
industry as a whole;
Moving Agile Beyond Software

- Prerequisites for building enterprise
  software

  - Identify initiatives
  - Business case
  - Funding
  - Resources
  - Business objectives
  - Architecture and others

- There is scope for expanding the role of
  agile to other broader areas

however, the question that looms large in front
of us is, is that sufficient? Or in other words, is
this scope to turn off these values and principles
beyond the immediate context of software

development? Even considering only software development, and even if the development team does follow agile methods, in a traditional enterprise, a law needs to be in place before a single line of code can be written. At a minimum, initiatives need to be identified, business case needs to be established, funding needs to be arranged, resources, which include human and other kinds of resources, need to be identified and allocated, business objectives and high-level architecture need to be established. If you expand your examination to other areas outside software development, such as project management, portfolion management, change management, ID infrastructure, maintenance, support, and so forth. Except in a very small presentation of organizations, you would find that the processes in these domains are typically still stuck in there, highly stage-gated, waterfall-like, rigid processes, and suddenly, it seems like we have only scratched the surface of the potential that agile brings to an organization. There definitely seems to be scope, and as we will see subsequently, some urgent needs to scale agility from limited confines of software development to other broader areas.

Evolving Agile Manifesto

Given that prospective, there seems to be some room to relook at the agile manifesto for evolving it as a manifesto for agile enterprise, rather than confining its scope to software development only. Let's examine each value inshrined in the Agile Manifesto.

Individuals and Interactions Over Processes and Tools

- The right approach to knowledge work within a team

  - Can good/ productive interactions occur without a unifying vision to guide them?
  - Can teams play their roles effectively without the larger context?
  - Can teams effectively collaborate without knowing the dependencies and constraints that operate across teams?

"Establishing shared vision and strategy which sets the context for individuals and interactions within a team over following processes systematically"
Individuals and interactions over processes and tools. Well, that is the right principle to guide knowledge work within a team anyway; however, can good and productive interactions occur within a team, if it is not guided by the larger context that is part of? If the teams do not have awareness and clarity on which part of the vision they are trying to fulfill and the exact relationship that their outcomes would those of the outcomes produced by other teams, how can we even hope to align these outcomes within a larger scheme? Hence, could we rephrase this value along the following lines? Establishing shared vision and strategy, which sets the context for individuals and interactions within a team, over following processes systematically. Let's now look at the next value.

Working Software Over Comprehensive
Documentation

- Working software does not
  automatically result in business or
  customer outcome

  - Working software cannot be the
    end goal for an enterprise –
    business outcomes are
  - Pursuing agility and efficiencies
    locally often fail to achieve
    effective enterprise outcomes

"Effective customer and business outcomes
over working software over comprehensive
documentation"
It is working software over comprehensive
documentation. That sounds perfectly
reasonable, but in the context of the enterprise,
working software, although important, is not
going to produce a business outcome or
customer outcomes all by itself, but rather,
working software is more often an enabler,
which needs to work alongside other
disciplines, such as change management, ID
infrastructure setup, project, product, and
portfolio management, vendors, sourcing, and
procurement teams, marketing and corporate
communications, and so on and so forth. It has
been the experience of many agile development
teams that in spite of the local efficiencies
achieved through an agile development
practice, mostly limited to development teams,
and when there are no measures taken for the
team to align to other teams and disciplines that
develops business outcomes, and when the
pursuit of local efficiency does not take into

account specific strategic objectives that needs to be met, it does not lead to an effective business outcome, hence we could reword the value as follows: Effective customer and business outcomes over working software over comprehensive documentation.
Customer Collaboration Over Contract Negotiation

- Implies on-going customer input, continuous feedback, prioritization and ability to course correct

    - Would work great only if the customers know what they want Strategic, Tactical and Operational context and priorities need to be set

"Establishing strategic, tactical and operational priorities and employing customer collaboration in the light of these priorities"
The next value is customer collaboration over contract negotiation. This value implies on-going customer input to support continuous feedback, prioritization, and book correction; however, in an enterprise, that would work great only if the customers know what they want in relation to all other initiatives that are going on are planned within the enterprise. This almost never is the case, even for small enterprise projects, hence it is is important to have a mechanism that establishes overall enterprise strategy and the strategic alignment of each specific initiative. It also important to take into account tactical and operational priorities put into those initiatives, hence what the enterprise context requires is establishing

strategic, tactical, and operational priorities and employing customer collaboration in the light of these priorities.
Responding to Change Over Following a Plan

- This is the very definition of agility

    - Enterprise agility means agility for the whole organization

"Responding to change holistically as an enterprise rather than taking a piecemeal approach to agility"
And the final value is responding to change over following a plan. Well, this is the very definition of agility; however, it is important to realize that enterprise agility implies agility for the whole organization, and in the enterprise context, there is more value to be unlocked by scaling agility to strategic planning, architecture, portfolio management, and program management layers, rather than focusing exclusively on software development. Hence, from that we could say, responding to change holistically as an enterprise, rather than taking a piecemeal approach to agility.
Summing Up

- Agility inherently applies to the whole of enterprise
- Agile manifesto for enterprise could read as below:

    - Establishing shared vision and strategy to set the context for individuals and interactions

- Effective customer and business outcomes over working software
- Customer collaboration in the light of strategic, tactical and operational priorities
- Responding to change holistically as an enterprise

To sum up, agility inherently belongs to the whole of enterprise. Agile manifesto needs to have all its values along the following lines, to accommodate the whole of enterprise context: establishing shared vision and strategy to set the context for individuals and interactions, effective customer and business outcomes over working software, customer collaboration in the light of strategic, tactical, and operational priorities, responding to change holistically as an enterprise, rather than taking a piecemeal approach to agility.

Forces Driving Enterprise Agility

- It is not the strongest of the species that survive, nor the most intelligent, but the one most responsive to change

"It is not the strongest of the species that survive, nor the most intelligent, but the one most responsive to change"- Leon Megginson. It is worth noting and keeping in mind this very insightful quote as we begin our quick exploration of the forces that are driving enterprises to embrace agility more holistically.

- Examine Principles in Agile Manifesto
- **Forces Driving Lean/ Scaled Agility**
- Impact on EA Practice
- What is Lean/ Agile Architecture?

Agility is the new refrain for the enterprise for various reasons. The drivers for enterprise agility can be broadly classified as top down and bottom up. Where the top down drivers are the macro factors, including the business landscape, macro trends in the economy and industry, and the bottom up drivers are the internal and inherent factors that drive the enterprises towards greater efficiency and effectiveness of its processes. Let's go through some statistics to introduce some of the macro trends in the industry. In an April 2011 article in Forbes, the contributor Nathan Furr outlined the challenge to big business survival. The article predicted that all of the Fortune 1000 companies that led the industry a mere 10 years ago, 70% will be replaced by 2013, and this has since been confirmed to be true by many independent sources. Overall, enterprise lifespans are shrinking. The data from Standards and Poors show that circa 1958, enterprises on an average had a lifespan of 61 years, while in 1980, this has been reduced to 25 years, and in 2012, further down to 18 years.

What Is Driving These Statistics?

- Empowered customers

  - Age of the customer is upon us

- Overwhelming levels of disruption

  - Continuous disruption is the key to survival

- Competitive business landscape

  - Entrepreneurship and innovation are vital

- Nature of workforce is shifting driven by knowledge economy

  - Knowledge work requires a deep cultural and paradigm shift

This, many experts believe are symptomatic of some underlined changes happening in the market place, which they believe are attributable to following factors: customers empowered by pervasive computing, connectivity and social media, have higher influence than ever before on market perception of a product or a grant, and hence, most enterprises require deeper engagement through close listening and adversity. It is quite literally true that the age of the customers is upon us. Overwhelming levels of disruptive technology innovations, powering disruptive business models are forcing large enterprises themselves to adopt disruption as a strategy. Emerging competitive business landscape driven by innovative, entrepreneurial, and fast-moving startups. Thanks to cloud technologies, smartphone equal systems, and impervious social media, these startups with the metaphoric dust under the stairway are empowered by easy and immediate accessibility to technology and a large, captive customer base. Such macro trends necessitates large enterprises to equally turn up their entrepreneurial and innovation process to stay relative and competitive. What places today are going through large-scale shift from predominately semi or unskilled workforce to a skilled knowledge-intensive workforce? Stephen Denning, in his book the Leader's Guide to Radical Management states that the onset of the knowledge economy, where knowledge-based work need to be performed by highly knowledgeable and skilled workforce has turned the situation topsy turvy, so to speak. For most of the previous centuries, the managers could tell the workers what to do and how to do their work, which they could not anymore in the knowledge-based work commandment. In the new and the evolving knowledge-based workplace, it becomes important for the knowledge workers to commit and engage in the work. The large-scale shift from repetitive and low-scaled work created knowledgable, demanding, corresponding shift in work culture and processes, and this requires a complete cultural and paradigm shift for how work is done at all layers of the organization, and hence, construed the key bottom of driver for the adoption of lean and agile practices within the enterprise. In summary, continuous and ongoing intitiatives are required to keep the customers delighted, which is an important requirement to succeed in the age of the customer. Quality products and incremental improvements are not differentiators anymore; they are a given. Enterprises are discovering that continuous customer delight is achievable only through insides, gathered from deeper engagement with customers and its ability to create adaptable differentiators through continuos disruptive innovation. So, how should an organization adapt to these changes? Well, a leading analyst of Forrester Research, Craig Le Claire puts it this way: agility could be what saves your enterprise. He says, in a world derived with change, dominance is not sustainable, only agility creates sustainable advantage. As we move forward, the market must put a premium on agility and companies must measure it along with other key metrics.

Impacts on Enterprise Architecture

- Examine Principles in Agile Manifesto
- Forces Driving Lean/ Scaled Agility
- **Impact on EA Practice**
- What is Lean/ Agile Architecture?

Now that we have briefly looked at the high-level forces driving changes into the enterprise space, let's now look at the impact this has on the tradition enterprise architecture practice. Enterprise Architecture Is Shifting Its Emphasis

- Enterprise agility
- Innovation

In general, the industry analysts believe that in addition to the roles already played by the enterprise architecture practice, which forms the blueprint for execution and change for the organization, the expectation and emphasis on the EA practice is gradually shifting towards the twin roles of enterprise agility and innovation. Enterprise agility is that capability that enterprise holds, that enable it to quickly rise up to and take requisite actions when the organization sends us opportunities and threats in the marketplace.

Enterprise Agility

- Embracing agility involves changes

    - Mindset
    - Culture
    - Organizational structures
    - Processes
    - And willingness to leverage technology

- Agility is part of the conversation today
- EA practice is expected to adapt and be an enabler of agility

Agility involves changes to mindset, culture, organizational structures, processes, as well as willingness to leverage technology that enables such capability. Agility is very much part of the conversations in the leading and forward-thinking enterprises of today, and the trend is on an upswing, hence, enterprise architecture practice is expected to adapt to this change, as well as become an enabler of such capability for the enterprise. And enterprise agility is increasingly intertwined with the digital transformation initiatives within the enterprise, which can be defined broadly as sweeping enterprise-wide initiatives that are leveraging existing technology, as well as new technology disruptions and paradigm shifts occurring in the industry to transform the digital customer experience. It also aims to achieve overall operational excellence, especially on processes that directly interfaces with or impacts on customers.

Digital Transformation

- Not surface level changes
- Often changes foundational business models
- Introduces sweeping changes

    - Across business units
    - Revamping systems, processes, interfaces
    - Renegotiating relationships, contracts and agreements
    - Technology footprint - refresh

- New refrain is "Build to evolve rather than to last"
- Enterprise Architects are called to shift their focus to rapidly building and configuring evolvable architectures for an agile enterprise

These are certainly deeper than surface level initiatives. They're not just about redesigning websites or changing the marketing slogans and content; it goes much deeper. In motion

sensors, these initiatives end up changing the foundational business model of the organization, thereby introducing sweeping changes across most of its business units. This may involve revamping systems, processes, internal and external interfaces, as well as renegotiating relationships, contracts, and agreements. Most such initiatives end up refreshing the overall technology footprint, as well, in order to support rapid
evolution and change of a business. The new refrain for the enterprise architecture, in general is to build to evolve, not to last. In order to support these transformation initiatives and the ongoing evolution of the enterprise and its platform of execution, enterprise architects are expected to transcend their traditional roles, which are primarily concentrated on enabling business ID alignment, setting technology standards, and enforcing the same. Towards becoming a facilitator and a value-added enabler of digital transformations in order to rapidly and responsibly create evolvable solutions for an agile enterprise. Let's now turn our attention to innovation. Responding quickly to threats and opportunites in order to stay competitive is important. It however represents only one side of the equation. Businesses that seek to create a truly sustainable advantage and market leadership must also innovate rapidly, continuously, and disruptively.

EA Enabling Disruptive Innovation

- Deep and broad knowledge of technology
- EA understands the platforms, data and information assets and their interconnections and their value

- Unique and holistic perspectives of business
- Trends in the industry and marketplace
- Holds deep connections within and outside the organization
- EA practice is uniquely positioned to catalyse disruptive business innovations

Enterprise architecture practice holds within that deep, as well as broad, knowledge of technology platforms, data, and information assets, powering radius business capabilities. They also have a good view on existing and potential interconnections between systems and the business and customer value that these interconnections represent. It also has unique and holistic perspectives of the business. EA practice is, in general, a rare of the trends prevalent in the marketplace, specific to the industry and across other industries. Another key asset of the EA practice are the connections and relationships that it maintains, but radius keys take orders at executive level and across radius business units, projects, and programs of work across the organization, as well as vendor organizations, suppliers, industry bodies, and so forth. With these attributes, the EA practice is uniquely positioned to catalyse disruptive business innovations enabled by technology. Summing Up

- Enterprise architecture is becoming an enabler of enterprise agility and innovation
- Enterprise agility and digital transformation are revamping enterprises rapidly

- Enterprise architecture is uniquely positioned to catalyze innovation within the enterprise

In summary, enterprise architecture practice is transitioning to become key enabler of enterprise agility and innovation. Enterprise agility and digital transformation initiatives are changing the fundamental business models, systems, processes, and technology for print of the enterprise. Enterprise architecture practice is uniquely positioned to play the role of a key enabler and a catalyst of innovation within the enterprise.

Understanding Agile Architecture 1

In his 1950 paper, Programing Computers to Play Chess, Claude Shannon presented some interesting numbers. He calculated that there are about nine million different possible positions on the board after three moves on each side. And the number of distinct 40-moves games possible is greater than the number of atoms in the observable universe. This kind of illustrates the power of emergence and the reason why it should be embraced and leveraged as a tool.

- Examine Principles in Agile Manifesto
- Forces Driving Lean/ Scaled Agility
- Impact on EA Practice
- **What is Lean/ Agile Architecture?**

In this final section of this module, we will look at what lean/agile architecture is. Before we begin, it's important to acknowledge that architecture is a collaborative initiative, and the practice of lean/agile architecture hinges on its environment, the values, the mindset, and the culture of the organization, as well as on active execute of support for establishing a lean/agile mindset and the supporting processes. The underlying assumption here is that the organization has already embraced some form of lean and scale agile practice, and we will focus on how architecture adapts to this mindset and way of working.

Lean/Agile Enterprise Architecture Value Chain

- Strategy Formulation

  - Architecture Development
  - Intentional Architecture

- Strategy Execution

  - Architecture Development
  - Emergent Architecture
  - Implementation Governance

- Operation

  - Governance (Change Management)

Overall, agile architecture value chain looks the same as the traditional value chain at a high level. If you zoom in closer, look at the actual enterprise architecture activities performed within each of these functions. You see that strategy formulation involves architecture development, and strategy execution involves both architecture development and implementation governance. The operate phase predominately involves governance and change management function. Now the key differentiation that agile architecture introduces is that it supports two kinds of architecture work: the intentional architecture and the emergent architecture. Strategy formulation predominately requires intentional architecture, while strategy execution involves more of emergent architecture. Let's look at why two different approaches are required to support architecture work and what value that adds overall.

Intentional Architecture

- Take long term views
- Look at wide landscape
- Articulate Enterprise-wide architectural vision
- Strategic architecture roadmap
- Architectural building blocks
- Logical view of architectural city-scape
- High-level architecture for specific initiatives, supporting

  - Sizing
  - Estimation
  - Business case creation

Intentional architecture: this kind of architecture work involves looking ahead long-term and looking at the wide landscape of

strategic business needs of the organization, as well as looking at the trends in the industry and new and emerging technology disruptions to arrive at high-level enterprise-wide architectural vision, as well as to create strategic architecture roadmap to achieve that vision. This involves identifying architectural building blocks that would form the conceptual and logical view of how the architectural cityscape of your enterprise will be built out. Apart from the high-level cityscapes that support long term strategic vision of the business, you may also engage in the intentional architecture development in support of specific enterprise initiatives to arrive at sizing, estimation, and
creation of business case, etcetera. That then influences the go or no-go decision on that initiative.

Intentional Architecture

- Not cast in stone

  - Best effort architecture done at a point in time

  - Collection of light-weight forward thinking architectural views

  - Guides further architecture work closer to implementation

  - Informs, influences and shapes early decisions on various initiatives

- Provides a head-start to more detailed architecture work closer to implementation

  - Documents a point-in-time view of assumptions, issues and constraints

It is worth noting that intentional architecture is not cast in stone; it is only a collection of light-weight, high-level architectural views. It is a best effort architecture created at a point in time by architects who understand the technology, the industry, and the domain, as well as the organization and its strategy. This is an early and forward-thinking view of the architecture landscape, which is intended to provide reference and guidance and act as pointers to drive further architectural work closer to implementation. The early and upfront intentional architecture also informs, influences, and shapes various decisions by identifying dependencies, constrains, and relationships among various architecture and business initiatives. This forms the high-level architecture defined from an anticipatory and forward-thinking perspective, thereby providing a head start for more detailed architecture work. Since it is forward-thinking and anticipatory in nature, it is heavy on assumptions and calls out potential risks and issues that need to be factored in.

Emergent Architecture

- Developed closer to implementation
- Architecture emerges

- Influenced by many operating factors
- Leverages the intentional architecture
- Validates intentional architecture
- Keeps the architectural vision alive

Emergent architecture, which forms part of the strategy execution is the architectural effort that is undertaken closer to implementation timeframe. Like in the game of chess, where the direction the game would take is unpredictable and hinges on the decision made by both players in each subsequent move, the final architecture that gets implemented cannot be predicted in advance. It emerges as a result of and at the intersection of conversations between and among architects and the collaborating stakeholders. It is influenced by their knowledge and awareness, their priorities, political influences, various forms of constraints, threat perceptions, regulatory regimes, and many other factors. Emergent architecture uses the early work done by the intentional architecture as a base line and the starting point for its efforts; however, it validates these assumptions and enables a final decision to be taken closer to implementation, based on real factors that are at play. However, it still keeps the decisions and choices in alignment with the architectural vision and in-sync with the strategic objectives. Let's examine why you need to engage in both intentional and emergent architecture development.

Comparing Architecture to Road Trip

- Identify the routes you can take
- Your choices vary based on many factors and trade off decisions

- This stage of planning is similar to intentional architecture

  - It helps you think ahead
  - Consider the options available to you
  - Make informed decisions in advance
  - Help you make best use of opportunities along the way
  - Prepares you better for the day of the journey

- Emergent architecture is like the decisions you take on the day of journey
- Both Intentional and Emergent Architectures are important and they complement each other

Let me use an analogy here. Let's assume that you're planning a road trip, which involves driving several days, and let's say you have never driven to this destination before, and you're not sure about the road you should be taking. The first logical step is to consult a map to figure out the roads that you can take. Your choices vary based on many factors and trade-offs, such as are you traveling with a group of friends or are you traveling as a family, are you taking any kinds on the trip? What are the special needs of the people that are traveling with
you that you want to accommodate? Can you take your car on the trip or will you rent one? You may want to consider the trade-offs between taking a toll road versus non-toll road,

total traveling distance on each route, the time it takes, the typical traffic impeding the time of travel, the scenic drives you may want to include on your route, or other points of interest that you may want to cover off. This is essentially what intentional architecture does. It helps you to think ahead and effectively prepare you in advance and arm you with reliable options, thus helping you make effective choices and informed decisions, and plan to take advantage of opportunities on route to your destination, while emergent architecture are the decisions that you take on the day of your travel. Based on the situations that you pursue on the ground and as situations emerge as you move ahead with your plan. Maybe the weather is not like what you expected. Maybe you came to know, while on the road, that a certain route is closed for some reason or there is way too much traffic condition on the road than you had anticipated. Given the current context, you may change parts of your plan to best suit your needs at that time and still adhere as much as you can to fulfill the objectives that you have set up for the trip. Both intentional and emergent architectures are important, and they compliment each other.

To Sum-up

- Architecture is both intentional and emergent
- Intentional architecture establishes the landscape
- Supports high-level decision making
- Head-start for detailed architecture work
- Emergent architecture provides context rich guidance

- Affordance to allow architecture decisions to be delayed
- Emergent architecture is roll-up your sleeves, collaborative kind of architecture

To sum-up, from a lean/agile view point, architecture development is both intentional and emergent in nature. Intentional architecture establishes the architectural landscape. It supports early high-level decision making, gives a head-start for detailed architecture work closer to implementation. Emergent architecture provides continuous context-rich guidance closer to implementation timeframe. Emergent architecture affords some key decisions to be delayed, the more delayed, higher the probability of it being more informed and more relevant and be able to leverage most opportunities. Emergent architecture is collaborative and involves rolling up your sleeves and working with the emerging scenarios.

Understanding Agile Architecture 2

"In preparing for battle, I have always found that plans are useless, but planning is indispensible. " -Dwight D. Eisenhower. Let's try and get a quick perspective on strategy as it relates to lean/agile architecture.
What Exactly Is Strategy?

- A very high level plan

- How an enterprise organizes its people and resources to fulfil its vision
- Drives many layers of detailed plans

- Strategy Themes define broad areas of focus

  - Typically the top 5 areas of focus for the enterprise

- Strategic objectives adds specificity

  - Strategic outcomes/ results further defines each objective

- Strategic objectives are mapped to enterprise initiatives managed by Enterprise Project Portfolio Management

  - Initiatives can be categorized as business and architecture initiatives

- Strategy promotes the lean/agile values of focus and effectiveness

What exactly is strategy? What is the simplest way to understand it? If you break it down, it simply is a very high-level plan. From an enterprise's perspective, a strategy is a high-level plan that shows how it will organize and mobilize the people and resources it has in order to fulfill its vision. This high-level plan drives many layers of lower-level that is more detail-oriented plans. Strategy usually gets expressed in the form of strategic themes, which can be defined as those broad areas of focus that an enterprise would pursue or engage in, in order to realize its vision. In order to keep it lean and focused, and in the interest of simplicity, these typically tend to be the top five focus areas. It does not have to be exactly five, but let's say it is usually around that number. At the level of strategic themes, the enterprise strategy is quite broad and lacks specificity, hence specific strategic objectives are identified, which are further annotated using what is referred to as strategic outcomes and results. Each strategic objective usually gets mapped to one or more large enterprise initiatives, through which these objectives can be fulfilled. Typically, these initiatives can be categorized as business initiatives and architecture initiatives. Architecture initiatives are usually built out in advance of and in order to support business initiatives. Strategy promotes the lean/agile values of focus and effectiveness at all levels of the enterprise. Let's now visualize this and briefly see how strategy gets articulated for an enterprise.

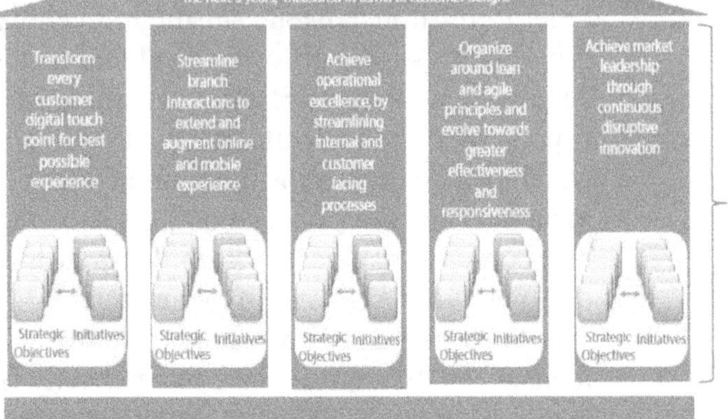

Let's now look at a hypothetical strategy for a retail bank, whose vision is to be the number one retail bank in their co-markets, within the next three years, measured in terms of customer delight. Based on its analysis, the bank has identified five key areas that it needs to focus on to achieve this vision, which are transform every customer digital touch point for best possible customer experience, streamline branch interactions to extend and augment online and mobile experience, achieve operational excellence by streamlining internal and customer facing processes, organize around lean and agile principles and evolve towards greater effectiveness and responsiveness, achieve market leadership through continuos, disruptive innovation. These five load-bearing pillars represent the strategic themes that the bank will focus on. Within each theme, the strategy identifies specific strategic objectives, which gets mapped to enterprise initiatives. As you can see, there are two kinds of initiatives: the blue color represents the business initiatives and the red color represents the architecture initiatives. The strategy is supported and enabled by the enterprise's values and cultures and active support from executive management. How did initiatives get ruled out in a lean/agile fashion? How does architecture participate in this process? Depending on the agile framework on methodology being implied caused scaling agility, usually the following pattern is played out in most agile enterprises. The enterprise initiatives are prioritized and sequenced and ordered in a central enterprise-wide receptacle maintained for the purpose.

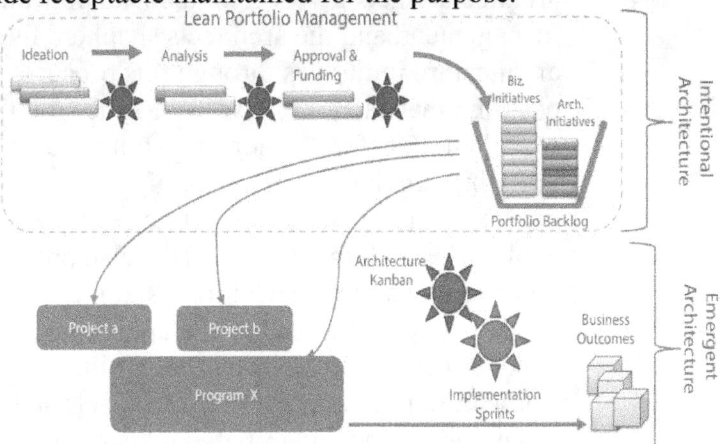

Some framework, such as safe, which is a scale agile framework, refers to these as portfolio backlog. Some enterprises may have separate backlogs for business initiatives versus for architecture initiatives. Some very large conglomerates that have business units that don't have much in common may choose to have several portfolios. This receptacle basically acts as a hand-off point between intentional and emergent architecture streams of work. To get to this backlog, each initiative transitions through a lean collaborative process flow. Lean techniques such as Kanban may be employed to transition these initiatives from its identification or ideation through various stages, including business case development and analysis, which include technical feasibility, sizing, identification of dependencies, constrains, and issues, as well as cost estimations. This is then followed by endorsement of the proposal to develop this initiative, which also involves a sign-off on the light-weight business case and architecture, which then is followed by approval and funding. This light-weight process is referred to as lean portfolio management. Enterprise architecture gets involved in the lean portfolio management, and the architects shepherd the architecture initiatives through this process, ensuring that each initiative is in-sync with the overall architectural vision and strategy as it goes through the process, as well as progressively flushing the architecture out as it evolves through the process. This also provides architectural and technical inputs to the executive decision makers and approvers to make effective decisions on these initiatives. These initiatives are mapped to projects and programs funded and initiated by enterprise portfolio management. Emergent architecture essentially occurs in the context of the specific project or program and usually involves architecture and design efforts that run in advance of the implementation's sprints. These architecture and design efforts can themsleves be organized in the form of Kanban flow or agile sprints.

Understanding Agile Architecture 3

The high-level lean/agile pattern does go so far works great for architecting large enterprise initiatives. It supports both intentional and emergent architecture work, but what about the more radical and disruptive innovations that we spoke about earlier in the module?

Innovation Value Chain

Harvest Ideas -->> Analyse/ Filter/ Prioritize -->> Experiment -->> Transition

A number of organizations are establishing, are already running innovation helps, whose value chain incorporates four major stages, including harvesting ideas for innovation enclosed in the entire organization, run an ideal's clearing-house to analyze, filter, and prioritize in order that the resources of the innovation team are spent to work on the most promising ideas. Run an experimentation lab to double-look and validate these ideas by bringing to life and testing them with real customers. Then, to transition these ideas into mainstream products and services. The executive management has a key role to play in bringing the innovation culture to all parts of the organization, encouraging and incentivising employees to think out of the box and to come up with bright ideas. This is often operationalized through a function headed by the chief innovative officer.

Analysis & Filtering of Ideas

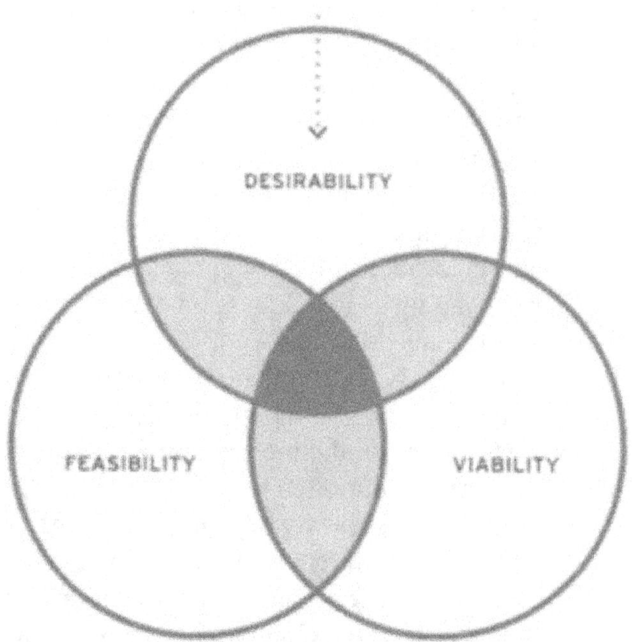

The analysis typically looks for ideas that falls within the Goldilocks zone of design-ability, technical, architectural, and business feasibility, as well as business reliability.

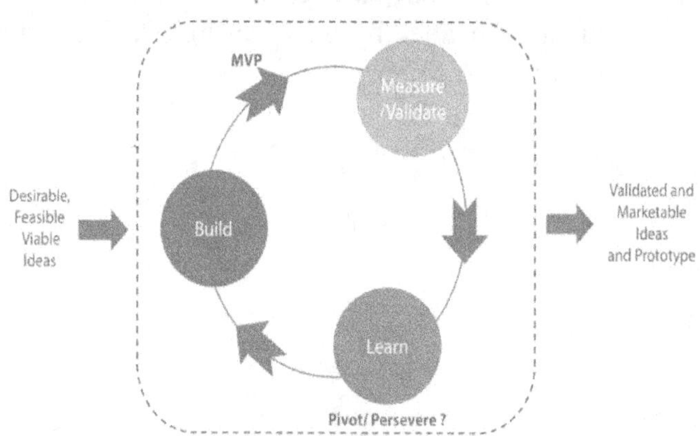

The experimentation states cycles are increasingly inspired by the lean start-up moment. It involves a small team comprised of internal entrepreneurs who typically use short iteration referred to as the build-measure-learn cycle suggested by the lean start-up approach to build the identified ideas into what is referred to as a minimum viable product, and then validate what they have built by actually letting real customers or customer representatives within the organization use these products. The team collects valuable learnings from watching the customers use the product and from listening to their reactions, comments, and feedback. At the end of each build-measure-learn iteration, the team accumulates enough learning to make the pivot or persevere decision. A pivot decision implies that the team decides to alter the original idea to align with what they have learned so far or in some cases, decide to abandon the work and focus on some other idea which seems more relevant or viable. To persevere of imply that the MVP or the minimum viable product, has perked some positive customer interest and acceptance and the team census promise in pursuing the idea further. A few iterations over the build-measure-learn feedback cycle results in validated, marketable idea for a product with the working prototype to give the development teams a head start.

Transition

The promising product ideas, along with early prototypes created through the build-measure-learn iterations can then be integrated into the lean portfolio management process described earlier to transition the product to mainstream development. What role does the enterprise architect play in this process? Here is a quick snapshot.

- Enterprise Architects are expected to be innovating futurists
- Functions as catalysts for innovation
- Influences the innovation clearing-house in the filtering and prioritization of ideas
- EA consults for and mentors innovation teams
- EA helps the transition from viable ideas into mainstream development

First and foremost, enterprise architects themselves function as an innovating futurist for the organization. They are expected to be constantly on the lookout for what is trending and the opportunities for potential market differentiation and customer delight, as well as keep a close watch on trends that the enterprise somehow missed out, and hence identify the best book of action to incorporate these. The enterprise architecture practice, as a whole, and the individual architects are expected to be the champions and catalysts of innovation across the organization to support the executive management and innovation team to establish a culture of innovation within the organization and use their wide network and influence to help harvest innovative ideas from the entire organization. The enterprise architecture practice uses the knowledge of business and technology landscape to consult, as part of the innovation clearing-house within the enterprise, that identifies potential business innovations and breakthrough ideas, prioritizing, sequencing, and filtering them, as well as fitting them into the strategic roadmap of the organization. Mentor, as well as consult, for the innovation teams through all their build-measure-learn cycles. With their footprint on the innovation space and the mainstream product development space, EA helps the transition of promising and viable ideas into mainstream agile product development cycle. That brings us to the end of this module.

Module Summary

- Examined agile manifesto for software development
- Identified ways in which the manifesto could be evolved to support agile enterprise
- Explored macro factors impacting enterprises and understood the rationale for rapid adoption of agility and innovation by the enterprise
- Examined the impact on enterprise architecture practice and how it is transitioning to become a key enabler of agility and innovation
- Identified what constitutes agile enterprise architecture
- Explored how enterprise architecture role fits within the agile scheme of things

Let's quickly summarize what we covered in this module. We began by exploring agile manifesto, as applicable to software development and identified ways in which the manifesto could be evolved to support agile enterprise. We looked closely at the macro factors impacting enterprises and understood the rationale for why forward-thinking enterprises are adopting a culture of agility and innovation. We then looked at, specifically, how enterprise architecture practice is transitioning to become a key enabler of agility and innovation within the organization. We then looked at what agile architecture means and how the enterprise architecture practice would typically work within a lean/agile enterprise.

www.ingramcontent.com/pod-product-compliance
Lightning Source LLC
Chambersburg PA
CBHW071931150726
47999CB00001B/179